THE POWER OF DISCIPLINE

Mastering Self-Control and Willpower for Success

Benjamin M. Noynay

BMN PUBLISHING

Copyright © 2025 by Benjamin M. Noynay

All rights reserved.

No portion of this book may be reproduced in any form without written permission from the publisher or author, except as permitted by Australian copyright law.

This publication is designed to provide accurate and authoritative information in regard to the subject matter covered. It is sold with the understanding that neither the author nor the publisher is engaged in rendering legal, investment, accounting, or other professional services. While the publisher and author have used their best efforts in preparing this book, they make no representations or warranties with respect to the accuracy or completeness of the contents of this book and specifically disclaim any implied warranties of merchantability or fitness for a particular purpose. No warranty may be created or extended by sales representatives or written sales materials. The advice and strategies contained herein may not be suitable for your situation. You should consult with a professional when appropriate. Neither the publisher nor the author shall be liable for any loss of profit or any other commercial damages, including but not limited to special, incidental, consequential, personal, or other damages.

Book Cover by BMN Graphics

First edition 2025

Contents

Introduction	IV
1. The Transformative Power of Discipline	1
2. The Science behind Discipline	33
3. Nurturing Discipline	67
4. Discipline and Time Management	102
5. Mastering Delayed Gratification	138
6. Overcoming Obstacles and Staying Committed	161
7. The Impact of Discipline on Personal and Professional Growth	174
8. The Long Road to Success	187
9. Building a Legacy Through Discipline	199
10. Embracing Discipline as a Lifelong Journey	210
Conclusion	217
About the author	219

Introduction

The word "discipline" evokes feelings of both respect and fear. It includes a collection of ideas and methods that have the power to change people's lives and result in outstanding accomplishments and personal development. Fundamentally, discipline is the ongoing commitment to self-control, consistency, and order. It is the capacity to overcome obstacles and put long-term objectives ahead of whims.

Discipline is essential for influencing our results and deciding the course of our lives, both personally and professionally. Discipline is the cornerstone of success and propels extraordinary accomplishments. People who are disciplined are better able to stay committed and focused, and they get past challenges in their pursuit of excellence.

Discipline becomes even more important in a world full of distractions and instant gratification. It serves as a compass that helps us stay on course and avoid getting sidetracked by fleeting desires or disappointments. Without discipline, dreams remain unrealized, and success becomes elusive.

We can grow and develop personally because discipline provides us the framework and structure we need. It establishes the routines and habits that promote advancement, enabling us to continuously move closer to our objectives. It is the instrument that allows us to maximize every opportunity by optimizing our time, resources, and talents.

Furthermore, discipline is not exclusive to any one area of life. It has an effect on relationships, general satisfaction, and personal well-being in addition to professional accomplishments. People who practice discipline are better able to control their thoughts, feelings, and behaviors, which improves their capacity to live meaningful lives and make thoughtful decisions.

By forcing people to step outside of their comfort zones, discipline acts as a catalyst for personal development. It inspires them to rise to challenges, endure hardship, and never stop trying to become better. People reach new levels of achievement and self-realization when they use discipline as their compass.

We set out to investigate the advantages of discipline in this book. We will explore methods for cultivating self-control and willpower, discuss the psychology of discipline, and look at how it affects different facets of life. With the help of real-world examples and useful insights, we will discover how to use discipline as a powerful tool for achievement and personal development.

As we embark on this journey, let's embrace the profound significance of discipline and the opportunities it offers. Developing discipline can lead to a life filled with fulfillment, success, and purpose. Let's explore discipline in greater detail and discover the enormous potential it has to influence our lives.

Chapter 1

The Transformative Power of Discipline

Exploring its Role in Achieving Success

The Benefits of Discipline

Discipline is more than just a concept; it is a powerful tool that brings forth numerous benefits and positive outcomes. By embracing discipline in our lives, we can experience increased productivity, enhanced focus, and improved efficiency. Additionally, discipline empowers us to manage our time effectively and achieve our goals with greater success and satisfaction. Let us have a closer look at each benefit.

Increased Productivity

Discipline acts as a catalyst for productivity. When we cultivate discipline, we develop the ability to prioritize tasks, eliminate distractions, and maintain a structured approach to our work. This heightened focus allows us to channel our energy and efforts towards the most important and impactful activities, leading to increased productivity and output.

Enhanced Focus

Discipline fosters laser-like focus. By adhering to disciplined practices, we train our minds to concentrate on the task at hand, minimizing the influence of external distractions. This deep focus enables us to analyze our work with undivided attention, leading to heightened levels of concentration and improved quality of output.

Improved Efficiency

Discipline brings efficiency to our actions. By establishing disciplined routines and approaches, we optimize our processes, eliminating unnecessary steps and reducing wasted time and effort. This streamlined approach enhances our efficiency, allowing us to accomplish tasks more effectively and with greater ease.

Effective Time Management

Effective time management closely intertwines with discipline. Through discipline, we develop the ability to prioritize our activities, allocate time wisely, and avoid procrastination. This skill enables us to make the most of each moment, ensuring that our time is utilized efficiently and effectively.

Goal Achievement

Discipline is essential for achieving our goals. By maintaining disciplined practices, we develop the perseverance and consistency necessary to work towards our objectives. Discipline keeps us focused on long-term aspirations, helping us overcome obstacles and stay committed to the actions required for goal attainment.

Greater Self-Control

Discipline strengthens our self-control and willpower. It equips us with the ability to resist immediate gratification and make choices aligned with our long-term objectives. This enhanced self-control empowers us to overcome temptations and impulses that may hinder our progress, leading to more informed and intentional decision-making.

Personal Growth and Development

Discipline is a catalyst for personal growth and development. By embracing discipline, we commit ourselves to continuous improvement and learning. It encourages us to engage in deliberate practice, develop new skills, and expand our knowledge, fostering personal growth in various areas of life.

Reduced Stress and Anxiety

Discipline contributes to reduced stress and anxiety levels. When we have disciplined routines and systems in place, we can manage our responsibilities more effectively, minimizing the likelihood of feeling overwhelmed or anxious. The structure and predictability that discipline provides can alleviate stress, creating a sense of calm and control.

Improved Health and Wellness

Discipline extends to our health and wellness. By adopting disciplined habits, such as regular exercise, balanced nutrition, and sufficient rest, we prioritize our well-being. Discipline supports the development of healthy lifestyle choices, contributing to improved physical and mental health.

Sense of Accomplishment and Fulfillment

Discipline brings a sense of accomplishment and fulfillment. As we adhere to disciplined practices and witness the progress we make, we experience a deep sense of satisfaction and pride. Investing consistent effort and commitment through discipline leads to a greater sense of purpose and fulfillment in our endeavors.

Discipline as a Foundation for Success

Discipline serves as a solid foundation for success, providing the structure and mindset necessary to achieve long-term goals. It is the constant dedication to self-control, consistency, and perseverance that propels individuals towards success.

By embracing discipline, individuals lay the groundwork for their journey towards their aspirations, encouraging an intense sense of resolve and resilience.

Establishing Long-Term Goals

Discipline enables individuals to set and pursue long-term goals effectively. It provides the focus and commitment needed to define clear objectives and develop a roadmap for achieving them. Even in the face of challenges or setbacks, discipline ensures individuals remain dedicated to their goals.

Cultivating Consistency

Discipline breeds consistency in actions and behaviors. It instills the habit of showing up, putting in the necessary work consistently, and maintaining a steady pace towards progress. Consistency, facilitated by discipline, allows individuals to build momentum and make gradual, sustainable strides towards their goals.

Developing Resilience

Discipline cultivates resilience in individuals. It teaches them to persevere through obstacles, setbacks, and failures. By maintaining discipline in the face of adversity, individuals develop the strength to bounce back, learn from their experiences, and continue moving forward, undeterred by temporary setbacks.

Strengthening Focus and Concentration

Discipline fosters enhanced focus and concentration. It helps individuals block out distractions, prioritize their efforts, and channel their energy towards the task at hand. Individuals can maintain unwavering focus and direct their efforts towards actions that truly matter when they have discipline as their foundation.

Instilling Effective Habits

Discipline empowers individuals to develop and maintain effective habits. It prompts individuals to establish routines that support their goals, such as consistent practice, deliberate learning, and productive habits. These disciplined habits create a supportive framework for success, automating positive behaviors that contribute to progress.

Overcoming Procrastination

Discipline helps individuals overcome procrastination. It allows them to resist the allure of instant gratification and instead prioritize long-term goals. Through disciplined practices, individuals develop the capacity to overcome the temptation to postpone tasks and take immediate action toward their objectives.

Nurturing Self-Control

Discipline nurtures self-control, which is essential for success. It strengthens the ability to make conscious choices aligned with long-term goals, resisting impulsive behaviors that may hinder progress. By developing self-control through discipline, individuals gain mastery over their actions and decisions.

Fostering Accountability

Discipline stimulates a sense of responsibility within individuals. It encourages them to take ownership of their actions, outcomes, and progress. By holding themselves accountable to disciplined practices, individuals ensure that they remain on track and actively take responsibility for their success.

Building a Strong Work Ethic

Discipline is synonymous with a strong work ethic. It instills a sense of commitment, diligence, and dedication towards one's endeavors. When discipline serves as the foundation, individuals develop the determination and drive to exert the necessary effort and exceed expectations to achieve their goals.

Sustaining Motivation

Discipline provides the necessary structure to sustain motivation over an extended period. While motivation may fluctuate, discipline remains constant. It serves as the driving force that keeps individuals focused and committed even during periods when motivation may wane. Discipline ensures that individuals stay on track, regardless of external factors, and continue progressing towards success.

Discipline forms the bedrock upon which success is built. By embracing discipline as a foundation, individuals establish the necessary mindset, habits, and practices to achieve their long-term goals. It fosters consistency, perseverance, resilience, and self-control, all of which are critical for dealing with the hardships and complexities of the success journey. By adopting discipline as their guiding principle, individuals can confidently pave their path towards realizing their aspirations.

Overcoming Procrastination and Building Discipline

Procrastination, often regarded as the nemesis of productivity, can obstruct progress and hinder the development of discipline. Recognizing common obstacles to discipline, such as procrastination and lack of motivation, is crucial for overcoming them. By implementing effective strategies, individuals can conquer procrastination and build the necessary foundation of self-discipline to achieve success.

Understanding Procrastination

Procrastination stems from various sources, including fear, perfectionism, overwhelm, or a lack of clarity. It is important to identify the underlying reasons behind procrastination and address them effectively.

Setting Clear Goals

Defined goals provide a sense of direction and purpose, reducing the likelihood of procrastination. By breaking down larger objectives into smaller, actionable tasks, individuals can create a roadmap that encourages consistent progress.

Prioritizing Tasks

Prioritization is key to overcoming procrastination. By determining the most important and urgent tasks, individuals can focus their energy on what truly matters, which minimizes the tendency to delay or avoid crucial responsibilities.

Creating Accountability Systems

Accountability systems can help individuals overcome procrastination. Such practices can include sharing goals with a trusted friend or mentor, joining an accountability group, or using productivity apps that track progress. Accountability enhances motivation and provides external support for maintaining discipline.

Implementing Time Management Techniques

Effective time management techniques, such as the Pomodoro Technique or time blocking, can combat procrastination. Breaking tasks into smaller, manageable intervals and setting aside dedicated periods for focused work can enhance both productivity and discipline.

Overcoming Perfectionism

Perfectionism often fuels procrastination. By adopting a mindset that values progress over perfection, individuals can overcome their fear of failing to meet impossibly high standards and take action towards achieving their goals.

Building Momentum

Getting started is often the hardest part. By committing to taking small, consistent steps towards a task, individuals can build momentum and find it easier to continue working while gradually developing their discipline.

Creating a Supportive Environment

Surrounding oneself with a conducive environment is vital for overcoming procrastination. Such practices can include minimizing distractions, organizing the workspace, and surrounding oneself with positive influences that encourage discipline.

Cultivating Self-Awareness

Developing self-awareness helps individuals understand their patterns of procrastination and the triggers that lead to avoidance. By recognizing these patterns, individuals can implement targeted strategies to counteract them and cultivate discipline.

Celebrating Progress

Celebrating achievements and milestones along the way can boost motivation and reinforce discipline. Recognizing progress, even in small increments, increases one's sense of achievement and fuels the drive to continue pushing forward.

Overcoming procrastination and building discipline requires consistent effort and a willingness to confront challenges head-on. By implementing strategies such as goal setting, prioritization, accountability, time management, and creating a supportive environment, individuals can overcome procrastination and build the foundation of discipline necessary for long-term success.

With patience, perseverance, and a commitment to personal growth, individuals can unlock their potential, accomplish their goals, and cultivate lasting discipline in their lives.

Discipline and Personal Development

A powerful symbiotic relationship intertwines discipline and personal development. Discipline serves as a catalyst for personal growth and self-improvement, while personal development enhances discipline. By cultivating discipline, individuals can experience significant advancements in various aspects of their lives, including acquiring new skills and fostering positive habits.

Commitment to Consistent Effort

Discipline entails commitment to consistent effort. Through disciplined practices, individuals develop the habit of dedicating regular time and energy towards their personal development goals. This commitment allows for continuous learning, skill acquisition, and progress.

Skill Acquisition and Mastery

Discipline provides the framework for skill acquisition and mastery. By adhering to disciplined routines and deliberate practice, individuals can effectively develop and refine their abilities. Discipline ensures that individuals consistently participate in focused, intentional learning and take the necessary steps to acquire new skills.

Building Positive Habits

Discipline plays a vital role in building positive habits. By establishing disciplined routines, individuals can embed positive behaviors into their daily lives. Whether it involves practicing self-care, maintaining a healthy lifestyle, or consistently engaging in activities that foster personal growth, discipline serves as the foundation for building and sustaining these habits.

Expanding Knowledge and Expertise

Discipline is the gateway to expanding knowledge and expertise. Through disciplined practices such as reading, research, and deliberate learning, individuals can broaden their intellectual horizons and deepen their understanding of various subjects. Consistently pursuing knowledge through discipline promotes personal development and intellectual growth.

Developing Self-Discipline

Personal development and self-discipline are inextricably linked. By cultivating discipline, individuals strengthen their self-discipline—the ability to regulate and control their thoughts, emotions, and actions. Self-discipline serves as a crucial skill in personal development, enabling individuals to make intentional choices and overcome obstacles on their path to growth.

Goal Orientation and Achievement

Discipline fuels goal orientation and achievement. Personal development often involves setting and pursuing specific goals. Discipline provides individuals with the focus, perseverance, and consistency necessary to remain dedicated to their goals while overcoming challenges and setbacks along the way.

Time Management and Productivity

Effective time management and increased productivity closely correlate with discipline. Adhering to disciplined practices allows individuals to optimize their time allocation towards activities that foster personal development. Discipline prevents time wastage and encourages individuals to prioritize their efforts to achieve maximum productivity.

Emotional Regulation and Resilience

Discipline fosters emotional regulation and resilience. Personal development requires navigating challenges and setbacks, which can evoke various emotions. Discipline equips individuals with the skills to manage and regulate their emotions, which enables them to recover from setbacks, maintain focus, and continue their journey of personal growth.

Empowering Self-Reflection

Discipline encourages self-reflection. By incorporating disciplined practices such as journaling or mindfulness, individuals create space for introspection and self-awareness. Self-reflection fosters personal growth by helping individuals gain insights into their strengths, areas for improvement, and values, which allows for intentional development.

Cultivating a Growth Mindset

Discipline cultivates a growth mindset—the belief that abilities and intelligence can be developed through effort and dedication. Personal development thrives on a growth mindset, which encourages individuals to embrace challenges, learn from failures, and persist in their pursuit of self-improvement.

Discipline and personal development are inseparable companions on the journey of self-improvement. By embracing discipline, individuals can unlock their potential, acquire new skills, develop positive habits, and foster personal growth. Through consistent effort, commitment, and a focus on intentional development, individuals can cultivate lasting discipline and experience transformative personal growth.

The Link between Discipline and Willpower

Willpower and discipline closely collaborate to foster personal growth and success. Understanding the connection between discipline and willpower is essential for harnessing their combined strength and utilizing both effectively.

Definition of Willpower

Willpower refers to the ability to resist short-term temptations and impulses in order to achieve long-term goals. It involves self-control, determination, and the capacity to make conscious choices aligned with desired outcomes.

Role of Discipline in Strengthening Willpower

Discipline acts as a training ground for willpower. By consistently practicing discipline in various aspects of life, individuals enhance their ability to exercise self-control and resist immediate gratification. Discipline strengthens the willpower muscle, making it easier to make choices that align with long-term goals.

Building a Foundation of Discipline

Discipline serves as the foundation upon which willpower can flourish. By cultivating discipline through consistent routines, habits, and practices, individuals create a framework that supports the development of willpower. Discipline provides the structure and mindset necessary to make deliberate choices and maintain focus on long-term objectives.

Consistency and Persistence

Discipline cultivates consistency and persistence, which are vital components of willpower. Through disciplined practices, individuals learn to stay committed and persevere in the face of challenges and distractions. The ability to maintain consistency and persistence builds the resilience needed to exert willpower effectively.

Strengthening Self-Control

Discipline plays a crucial role in strengthening self-control, a fundamental aspect of willpower. By consistently practicing self-control in various areas of life, individuals enhance their ability to make conscious decisions and resist impulses that may hinder progress towards long-term goals. Discipline provides the foundation for developing and exercising self-control effectively.

Reinforcing Motivation

Discipline reinforces motivation, a key driver of willpower. By establishing disciplined routines and habits, individuals create an environment that sustains motivation over the long term. The consistent practice of discipline keeps individuals focused and committed, ensuring that motivation remains high even when faced with challenges or setbacks.

Overcoming Temptations and Distractions

Discipline empowers individuals to overcome temptations and distractions that can erode willpower. By practicing discipline, individuals develop the ability to resist immediate gratification and stay focused on their long-term objectives. Discipline enables individuals to navigate temptations and distractions more effectively, preserving and strengthening willpower.

Developing a Strong Mindset

Discipline contributes to the development of a strong mindset, which is essential for harnessing willpower. Through disciplined practices, individuals cultivate resilience, determination, and a growth-oriented mindset. This mindset provides the mental fortitude needed to make difficult choices and persevere, bolstering willpower.

Mutual Reinforcement

Discipline and willpower reinforce each other in a reciprocal relationship. As discipline strengthens willpower, the presence of willpower further enhances discipline. The combined force of discipline and willpower creates a positive feedback loop, leading to increased self-control, consistency, and success.

Sustaining Long-Term Commitment

Discipline and willpower work together to sustain long-term commitment. Discipline provides the structure and habits that support consistent effort, while willpower enables individuals to stay committed and make choices aligned with their long-term goals. The symbiotic relationship between discipline and willpower ensures that individuals maintain their commitment over time, overcoming obstacles and achieving success.

Discipline and willpower are interconnected forces that drive personal growth and achievement. Discipline serves as the foundation for building willpower, enhancing self-control, and fostering consistency. Willpower, in turn, strengthens discipline by reinforcing motivation, enabling individuals to overcome temptations, and sustaining long-term commitment. By understanding and harnessing the link between discipline and willpower, individuals can unlock their full potential, make conscious choices, and pursue their goals with utmost loyalty.

Cultivating Discipline in Daily Life

Discipline is not merely a concept; it is a practice that can be cultivated and integrated into daily life. By incorporating discipline into our routines and habits, we can create a structured and focused approach to daily activities. Here are practical tips for cultivating discipline in everyday life:

Set Clear Goals

Begin by setting clear and specific goals for different areas of your life. Clearly defined goals provide a sense of direction and purpose, serving as a compass for your actions.

Create a Daily Schedule

Establish a daily schedule that includes dedicated time blocks for important activities. This trait helps prioritize tasks, ensures proper time management, and reduces the likelihood of procrastination.

Start with Small Steps

Build discipline gradually by starting with small, achievable tasks. Breaking down larger goals into smaller, manageable steps makes them less overwhelming and increases the likelihood of success.

Practice Time Management

Effective time management is crucial for cultivating discipline. Set deadlines, prioritize tasks, and allot time for specific activities. Avoid distractions and stay focused on the task at hand.

Develop Consistent Routines

Create consistent daily routines that support your goals and priorities. By incorporating regular practices into your routine, such as exercise, meditation, or reading, you build discipline through consistent repetition.

Embrace Accountability

Find ways to hold yourself accountable for your actions. Share your goals with a trusted friend, join an accountability group, or use productivity apps that track your progress. Accountability fosters discipline by providing external support and motivation.

Practice Self-Control

Discipline requires self-control and the ability to resist immediate gratification. Practice self-control by saying no to distractions, avoiding temptations, and making conscious choices aligned with your long-term goals.

Cultivate a Growth Mindset

Adopt a growth mindset, which focuses on learning and improvement. Embrace challenges, view setbacks as opportunities for growth, and approach tasks with a mindset of continuous learning and development.

Seek Support and Inspiration

Surround yourself with supportive individuals who encourage discipline and personal growth. Seek inspiration from books, podcasts, or mentors who exemplify discipline and provide guidance on your journey.

Reflect and Adjust

Regularly reflect on your progress and make necessary adjustments. Assess your habits, routines, and goals to ensure they align with your values and aspirations. Be willing to adapt and refine your approach to maintain discipline.

By incorporating these practical tips into your daily life, you can gradually cultivate discipline and make it an integral part of your routine. Consistent practice can develop discipline as a skill. Over time, you will experience the advantages of discipline in achieving your goals, enhancing productivity, and fostering personal growth.

Discipline and Decision-Making

Discipline plays a significant role in the decision-making process, influencing the quality of choices we make and the outcomes we achieve. By cultivating discipline, individuals develop the capacity to make informed decisions and exercise better judgment. Here's a comprehensive explanation of the relationship between discipline and decision-making:

Clarity and Focus

Discipline brings clarity and focus to the decision-making process. By practicing discipline, individuals develop the ability to prioritize, eliminate distractions, and stay focused on the relevant factors when making decisions. This enhances the clarity of thought and enables more effective decision-making.

Rationality and Objectivity

Discipline helps individuals approach decision-making with rationality and objectivity. By cultivating discipline, individuals learn to detach themselves from biases, emotions, and impulsive reactions. This allows for a more objective evaluation of options and consideration of the long-term consequences, leading to better decision-making.

Delayed Gratification

Discipline strengthens the ability to delay gratification, which is crucial in decision-making. Discipline empowers individuals to resist immediate but potentially detrimental rewards, opting instead for choices that align with long-term goals and values.

Consistency and Reliability

Discipline promotes consistency and reliability in decision-making. By developing disciplined habits and routines, individuals establish a structured approach to decision-making, ensuring that choices are based on consistent principles and values.

Enhanced Self-Control

Discipline enhances self-control, a critical aspect of decision-making. By practicing discipline, individuals strengthen their self-control, enabling them to resist impulsive or irrational choices. This self-control allows for more deliberate decision-making and reduces the likelihood of regrets.

Consideration of Consequences

Discipline encourages individuals to consider the potential consequences of their decisions. By practicing discipline, individuals develop the habit of assessing the short-term and long-term implications of their choices, making decisions that align with their goals and values.

Critical Thinking and Analysis

Discipline fosters critical thinking and analysis, essential skills in effective decision-making. By cultivating discipline, individuals train themselves to think critically, evaluate information, and consider multiple perspectives. This analytical approach enables more informed and well-thought-out decisions.

Patience and Reflection

Discipline promotes patience and reflection in decision-making. By practicing discipline, individuals learn to take the time to reflect, gather information, and carefully weigh options before making a decision. This patience allows for a more thorough evaluation and reduces the likelihood of impulsive or hasty choices.

Long-Term Orientation

Discipline encourages a long-term orientation in decision-making. By practicing discipline, individuals develop the capacity to consider the potential long-term impact of their decisions on their goals, values, and overall well-being. This long-term perspective fosters wiser decision-making.

Improved Decision-Making Skills

Ultimately, discipline enhances decision-making skills as a whole. By consistently practicing discipline, individuals develop a mindset and approach that supports effective decision-making. They become adept at gathering information, considering alternatives, and making choices aligned with their overall vision and objectives.

By cultivating discipline, individuals elevate their decision-making process. They gain the ability to approach choices with clarity, objectivity, and self-control. Discipline fosters critical thinking, consideration of consequences, and a long-term perspective, leading to more informed and impactful decisions. Through consistent practice, individuals can harness the power of discipline to make better choices and ultimately achieve their desired outcomes.

Discipline and Emotional Regulation

Discipline plays a vital role in emotional regulation, enabling individuals to effectively manage their emotions and cultivate resilience. The relationship between discipline and emotional control is multi-faceted, as discipline provides the framework and tools necessary to navigate and regulate one's emotional experiences. Here is a comprehensive explanation of how discipline contributes to emotional regulation and resilience:

Self-Awareness

Discipline fosters self-awareness, a key component of emotional regulation. By practicing discipline, individuals develop the ability to observe and understand their emotions, recognizing patterns and triggers that impact their emotional states. This self-awareness lays the foundation for effective emotional regulation.

Response vs. Reaction

Discipline empowers individuals to respond rather than react to emotional stimuli. Through disciplined practices, individuals learn to pause, assess the situation, and choose a thoughtful response, rather than being driven by impulsive reactions. This ability to respond consciously promotes emotional regulation.

Emotional Stability

Discipline promotes emotional stability by providing a sense of control and balance. By consistently practicing discipline, individuals develop the capacity to regulate their emotions and maintain stability even in challenging circumstances. This stability allows for more adaptive responses to emotional triggers.

Stress Management

Discipline supports effective stress management, a crucial aspect of emotional regulation. Through disciplined routines, individuals establish healthy coping mechanisms and stress reduction practices. Taking a proactive approach to stress management not only boosts emotional resilience but also lessens the risk of experiencing overwhelming emotions.

Cognitive Restructuring

Discipline contributes to cognitive structuring, which involves reframing and altering negative thought patterns. By practicing discipline, individuals cultivate the ability to challenge negative thoughts and replace them with more positive and constructive perspectives. This cognitive restructuring aids in emotional regulation by influencing one's emotional responses.

Impulse Control

Discipline strengthens impulse control, an essential skill for emotional regulation. By consistently practicing discipline, individuals enhance their ability to resist impulsive behaviors driven by intense emotions. This control allows for more intentional and balanced emotional responses.

Emotional Intelligence

Discipline fosters emotional intelligence, the ability to recognize and manage one's own emotions and empathize with others. By cultivating discipline, individuals develop the emotional intelligence necessary for understanding and regulating their emotions effectively. This promotes healthier emotional experiences and interactions with others.

Resilience Building

Discipline plays a pivotal role in building resilience, which is the ability to bounce back from adversity. By practicing discipline, individuals develop the resilience needed to cope with and recover from emotionally challenging situations. Discipline instills perseverance and determination in individuals, enabling them to navigate setbacks and emotional hardships with greater resilience.

Healthy Coping Mechanisms

Discipline encourages the development of healthy coping mechanisms to manage emotions. Instead of relying on unhealthy or destructive behaviors to cope with intense emotions, disciplined individuals are more likely to engage in positive coping strategies such as exercise, meditation, or seeking support from others. These healthy coping mechanisms help individuals manage their emotions effectively.

Emotional Well-Being

Ultimately, discipline contributes to overall emotional well-being. By practicing discipline, individuals create a foundation for emotional regulation, resilience, and positive emotional experiences. Discipline fosters a sense of control, balance, and self-mastery, which leads to greater emotional well-being and an improved overall quality of life.

Discipline and emotional regulation are interconnected, with discipline providing the tools and mindset necessary to effectively manage and regulate emotions. Through self-awareness, response rather than reaction, stability, stress management, impulse control, cognitive restructuring, emotional intelligence, resilience building, healthy coping mechanisms, and enhanced emotional well-being, discipline empowers individuals to navigate their emotions with greater control and resilience. By cultivating discipline, individuals can enhance their emotional regulation and achieve greater emotional balance and fulfillment.

Examples of Discipline in Action

Discipline is a transformative force that has the power to propel individuals to unparalleled heights of success and achievement. By examining real-life examples of individuals who have demonstrated exceptional discipline, we can learn important lessons about the power that transforms discipline. Here are inspiring case studies and examples of discipline in action:

Elon Musk

The visionary entrepreneur Elon Musk exemplifies discipline in action. Known for his relentless work ethic and unwavering focus, Musk has achieved remarkable success with ventures like SpaceX, Tesla, and Neuralink. His disciplined approach to setting ambitious goals, working long hours, and persevering through challenges has propelled him to become one of the most influential figures in technology and innovation.

Serena Williams

Serena Williams, a tennis legend, is a shining example of discipline in the realm of sports. Her rigorous training regimen, dedication to physical fitness, and relentless drive for excellence have made her one of the greatest tennis players of all time. Williams' unwavering discipline and commitment to continuous improvement have led to her winning numerous Grand Slam titles and making a lasting impact on the world of tennis.

Angela Duckworth

Angela Duckworth, a renowned psychologist, has conducted extensive research on the role of discipline in achieving success. Her groundbreaking work on grit, defined as a combination of passion and perseverance, highlights the power of discipline in long-term goal achievement. Through her research, Angela Duckworth has demonstrated how discipline and sustained effort contribute to high levels of achievement in various domains.

J.K. Rowling

J.K. Rowling, the author of the Harry Potter series, overcame numerous setbacks and rejections before achieving phenomenal success. Her disciplined approach to writing, characterized by a strict daily writing routine and a lifetime dedication to her craft, allowed her to bring her imaginative world to life. Rowling's story exemplifies the benefits of discipline when facing adversity.

Mahatma Gandhi

Mahatma Gandhi, the iconic leader of India's independence movement, embodied discipline in his pursuit of social and political change. His commitment to nonviolent resistance, self-discipline, and adherence to principles led to the successful achievement of India's independence. Gandhi's disciplined approach has inspired millions and continues to serve as a guiding light for those striving for positive change.

Michael Phelps

Michael Phelps, the most decorated Olympian in history, achieved his remarkable success through incredible discipline and dedication to his sport. His rigorous training regimen, strict diet, and never-ending dedication to excellence allowed him to dominate the world of swimming and win 23 Olympic gold medals. Phelps' story showcases the power of discipline in maximizing athletic potential.

Oprah Winfrey

Oprah Winfrey, a media mogul and philanthropist, has demonstrated discipline throughout her career. Her disciplined approach to self-improvement, personal growth, and professional development has propelled her from a challenging childhood to becoming one of the most influential personalities in the world. Winfrey's commitment to lifelong learning and self-discipline has enabled her to create an empire and inspire millions.

Nelson Mandela

Nelson Mandela, the iconic leader and symbol of the anti-apartheid movement in South Africa, demonstrated remarkable discipline during his years of imprisonment. His steadfast loyalty to his ideals, self-discipline, and focus on reconciliation laid the foundation for a peaceful transition to democracy in South Africa. Mandela's story exemplifies the power of discipline in pursuing a just and equitable society.

Marie Curie

Marie Curie, a pioneering physicist and chemist, exemplifies discipline in the field of scientific discovery. Her relentless dedication to research, disciplined work ethic, and perseverance in the face of adversity led to groundbreaking discoveries in the field of radioactivity. Marie Curie's disciplined approach to her work revolutionized scientific understanding and earned her multiple Nobel Prizes.

Arnold Schwarzenegger

Arnold Schwarzenegger, the iconic bodybuilder, actor, and politician, is a testament to discipline's transformative power. His disciplined training routine, focus on self-improvement, and tireless dedication allowed him to become a seven-time Mr. Olympia champion and a successful Hollywood actor. Arnold Schwarzenegger's story illustrates the remarkable achievements that discipline can bring across multiple domains.

These are just some of the case studies that highlight the diverse ways in which discipline can lead to extraordinary accomplishments. We shall mention more examples later in the book. Whether in the domains of entrepreneurship, sports, academia, activism, or personal growth, individuals who have achieved remarkable success share a common thread of discipline. Their stories inspire us to cultivate discipline in our lives, harnessing its transformative effects as we pursue our dreams and make a positive impact on the world.

Chapter 2

The Science behind Discipline

Exploring the Psychology of Self-Control and Success

By reviewing the science behind discipline and self-control, this chapter provides you with a more profound understanding of the psychological processes that influence our ability to maintain discipline. It explores topics such as willpower, ego depletion, habit formation, motivation, goal setting, self-monitoring, cognitive strategies, and resilience. Armed with this knowledge, you can gain insights into the psychological foundations of discipline and utilize evidence-based strategies to enhance their self-control and achieve long-term success.

Introduction to the Psychology of Self-Control

Self-control and discipline are essential psychological factors that contribute to personal growth, success, and well-being. The introduction to the psychology of self-control provides a comprehensive understanding of the fundamental principles and theories that underpin the concept of discipline. Here is a comprehensive explanation of the key aspects of self-control and discipline:

Definition of Self-Control

Self-control refers to the ability to regulate and manage one's thoughts, emotions, impulses, and behaviors in alignment with long-term goals and values. It involves making conscious choices and resisting immediate gratification in favor of more significant rewards or desired outcomes.

Theoretical Perspectives

The introduction explores various theoretical perspectives that shed light on the psychology of self-control. This includes the ego depletion theory, which suggests that self-control is a limited resource that can become depleted over time, and the strength model of self-control, which proposes that self-control can be strengthened through practice.

Executive Functions

Self-control is closely linked to executive functions, which are cognitive processes involved in goal-directed behavior, such as attention, inhibition, working memory, and cognitive flexibility. Understanding these functions reveals the psychological mechanisms underlying self-control.

Importance of Self-Control

Self-control is a key predictor of success in various life domains. It influences academic and career achievements, health and well-being, interpersonal relationships, and financial stability. The introduction illustrates the importance of self-control in fostering positive outcomes and minimizing impulsive and detrimental behaviors.

Delayed Gratification

Delayed gratification, the ability to resist immediate rewards for a greater future benefit, is a crucial aspect of self-control. The introduction discusses the famous marshmallow experiment by psychologist Walter Mischel, which demonstrated the importance of delayed gratification in predicting future success.

Self-Control and Emotion Regulation

Self-control plays a critical role in managing and regulating emotions. It enables individuals to respond to emotional triggers in a measured and constructive manner, rather than being driven by impulsive reactions. The introduction explores the connection between self-control and emotion regulation.

Self-Control and Decision-Making

Self-control influences decision-making processes by enabling individuals to make choices that align with their long-term goals and values. It helps overcome the influence of immediate desires or temptations and supports rational and informed decision-making.

Self-Control Training

The introduction discusses the potential for self-control training programs that aim to enhance individuals' self-control abilities. These programs often incorporate strategies such as goal setting, self-monitoring, cognitive restructuring, and practicing self-discipline in various areas of life.

Implications for Personal Growth and Well-being

Developing self-control and discipline has profound implications for personal growth and well-being. By improving self-control, individuals can foster healthier habits, make better choices, manage stress effectively, and achieve long-term goals, leading to greater life satisfaction and fulfillment.

Practical Applications

The introduction concludes by highlighting the practical applications of understanding the psychology of self-control. It provides a foundation for implementing strategies to enhance self-control in everyday life, such as creating effective routines, setting achievable goals, managing impulses, and developing resilience.

The introduction to the psychology of self-control illustrates the fundamental principles and theories underlying discipline and self-control. It explores the definition of self-control, theoretical perspectives, the role of executive functions, the importance of self-control in various domains, the connection between self-control and emotion regulation, its influence on decision-making, and the potential for self-control training. Understanding the psychology of self-control empowers individuals to cultivate discipline, make better choices, manage impulses, and ultimately lead more fulfilling and successful lives.

The Role of Willpower in Discipline

Willpower, often referred to as self-control or self-discipline, plays a crucial role in maintaining discipline. It is the ability to override immediate impulses and temptations in order to stay focused on long-term goals. This comprehensive explanation examines the concept of willpower as a limited resource and its impact on maintaining discipline:

Definition of Willpower

Willpower refers to the mental capacity to exert control over one's thoughts, emotions, and behaviors. It involves making conscious choices that align with long-term objectives, even in the face of immediate gratification or distractions.

Limited Resource Theory

The concept of willpower as a limited resource suggests that it can become depleted with use. Research has shown that engaging in self-control tasks depletes the cognitive resources associated with willpower, making subsequent acts of self-control more challenging.

Ego Depletion

Ego depletion is a phenomenon that occurs when individuals' self-control resources are depleted, leading to diminished willpower and a reduced ability to maintain discipline. This depletion can manifest as decreased persistence, increased susceptibility to temptations, and impaired decision-making.

Impact of Willpower Depletion on Discipline

Understanding the limitations of willpower helps individuals recognize the challenges they may face in maintaining discipline consistently. When willpower is depleted, individuals may be more prone to succumbing to immediate gratification, procrastination, or impulsive behaviors that undermine their long-term goals.

Strategies to Preserve Willpower

Recognizing the limited nature of willpower, individuals can employ strategies to conserve and replenish their self-control resources. This may involve optimizing physical and mental well-being, managing stress levels, practicing mindfulness or relaxation techniques, and creating supportive environments that reduce the need for constant self-control.

The Role of Habits

Habits can serve as a powerful ally in maintaining discipline, as they rely less on conscious willpower and become automatic behaviors. By establishing positive habits that align with desired outcomes, individuals can reduce their reliance on willpower and make disciplined choices effortlessly.

Setting Priorities and Simplifying Choices

To conserve willpower, it is essential to set clear priorities and simplify decision-making processes. By reducing the number of choices and focusing on what truly matters, individuals can allocate their limited willpower resources more effectively.

Strengthening Willpower through Practice

While willpower is a limited resource, it can be strengthened through practice and training. Engaging in regular self-control exercises, such as consistently resisting small temptations or gradually increasing the difficulty of self-discipline tasks, can enhance an individual's overall capacity for willpower.

Building a Supportive Environment

The environment plays a significant role in supporting or hindering willpower and discipline. Creating an environment that minimizes distractions, promotes healthy habits, and provides social support can alleviate the strain on willpower and facilitate the maintenance of discipline.

Cultivating Intrinsic Motivation

Intrinsic motivation, driven by personal values and a sense of purpose, can serve as a potent source of willpower and discipline. When individuals are genuinely passionate about their goals, they are more likely to exert sustained effort, even when faced with challenges or depleted willpower.

Understanding the role of willpower as a limited resource is critical to sustaining discipline. By recognizing the potential for willpower depletion, individuals can develop strategies to preserve and replenish their self-control resources. Emphasizing habits, setting priorities, strengthening willpower through practice, creating a supportive environment, and cultivating intrinsic motivation are key factors in optimizing willpower and maintaining discipline consistently. By harnessing the power of willpower and understanding its limitations, individuals can overcome obstacles, stay focused on their long-term goals, and achieve greater success in various aspects of life.

Ego Depletion and Self-Regulation

Ego depletion refers to the phenomenon where self-control resources become depleted over time, resulting in reduced willpower and diminished ability to maintain discipline. This comprehensive explanation explores the concept of ego depletion and its implications for maintaining discipline.

Definition of Ego Depletion

Ego depletion is a psychological concept that suggests that self-control draws from a limited pool of mental resources. Engaging in tasks that require self-control or willpower depletes these resources, making subsequent self-control tasks more challenging.

Depleting Self-Control Resources

Engaging in acts of self-control, such as resisting temptations, making decisions, or regulating emotions, consumes cognitive resources. These resources, often referred to as "ego strength," can become depleted, leading to ego depletion.

Cognitive and Physiological Processes

Ego depletion involves both cognitive and physiological processes. It affects executive functions, such as attention, inhibition, and decision-making, as well as physiological indicators like glucose levels, which play a role in self-control.

Implications for Maintaining Discipline

Ego depletion has serious consequences when it comes to maintaining discipline. As self-control resources become depleted, individuals may find it harder to resist immediate gratification, make disciplined choices, or stay focused on long-term goals, leading to lapses in maintaining discipline.

Factors Influencing Ego Depletion

Various factors can influence the extent of ego depletion, such as task difficulty, individual differences in self-control capacity, and personal stress levels. Difficult or demanding tasks, as well as ongoing stressors, can deplete self-control resources more quickly.

The Role of Rest and Recovery

Rest and recovery play a crucial role in replenishing depleted self-control resources. Taking breaks, engaging in activities that restore mental energy (e.g., relaxation techniques, mindfulness, leisure activities), and getting adequate sleep can help restore self-control capacity.

Effects on Decision-Making

Ego depletion can impair decision-making processes. When self-control resources are depleted, individuals may rely on cognitive shortcuts or make impulsive decisions instead of carefully considering long-term consequences, potentially undermining their ability to maintain discipline.

Strategies to Counteract Ego Depletion

To counteract ego depletion and maintain discipline, individuals can implement strategies such as prioritizing tasks that require self-control during times when resources are less likely to be depleted, breaking tasks into manageable parts, and practicing self-care to replenish mental energy.

Interaction with Environmental Factors

Environmental factors can impact ego depletion. For example, exposure to tempting stimuli or distracting environments can deplete self-control resources more quickly, making it harder to maintain discipline.

Enhancing Self-Regulation Skills

Recognizing the phenomenon of ego depletion, individuals can focus on enhancing self-regulation skills. This may involve cultivating habits, establishing effective routines, utilizing cognitive strategies (e.g., cognitive restructuring, mindfulness), and engaging in activities that support self-control and mental well-being.

Understanding ego depletion and its implications for maintaining discipline is crucial for effective self-regulation. By recognizing the limited nature of self-control resources and implementing strategies to counteract ego depletion, individuals can enhance their ability to maintain discipline, make better choices, and achieve their long-term goals. Managing rest, optimizing decision-making processes, considering environmental factors, and developing self-regulation skills are key elements in meeting the difficulties posed by ego depletion and maintaining discipline consistently.

The Power of Habits and Routines

Habits and routines play a pivotal role in cultivating discipline and maintaining consistent behavior. This comprehensive explanation explores the science behind habit formation and the benefits of establishing effective routines that foster discipline.

Habit Formation

Habits are automatic behavioral patterns that are formed through repetition and reinforcement. The brain develops neural pathways that make certain actions more efficient and automatic over time. Understanding the process of habit formation offers information about how habits can support discipline.

Cue, Routine, Reward Loop

The habit formation process is often described as a cue, routine, and reward loop. A cue triggers a habitual behavior, followed by the routine itself, and finally, the reward serves as reinforcement. By identifying and manipulating cues and rewards, individuals can shape their habits to align with disciplined behavior.

Neuroplasticity and Habit Formation

The brain's capacity for neuroplasticity allows it to rewire neural connections based on repetitive behaviors. As habits are reinforced, the associated neural pathways strengthen, making the behavior more automatic. Harnessing neuroplasticity enables individuals to develop new habits that support discipline.

Keystone Habits

Some habits have a ripple effect, known as keystone habits. Keystone habits are behaviors that, when cultivated, trigger a chain reaction of positive changes in other areas of life. By identifying and focusing on keystone habits, individuals can leverage their power to promote discipline in various aspects of life.

Establishing Effective Routines

Routines provide structure and consistency, which are essential for maintaining discipline. By establishing effective routines, individuals reduce decision fatigue, enhance productivity, and create a supportive environment that encourages disciplined behavior.

Benefits of Routines

Effective routines offer several benefits for cultivating discipline. They provide a sense of stability and predictability, reduce the reliance on willpower, optimize time management, and create a framework for prioritizing tasks. Routines also facilitate the formation of positive habits by embedding desired behaviors into daily life.

Implementation Intentions

Implementation intentions are specific plans that link situational cues with intended actions. By formulating implementation intentions, individuals pre-plan their responses to potential challenges or temptations, enhancing their ability to maintain discipline in the face of distractions.

Habit Stacking

Habit stacking involves attaching a new habit to an existing one, leveraging the automaticity of an established habit to support the development of a new one. By stacking a desired disciplined behavior onto an existing routine, individuals can reinforce discipline without relying solely on willpower.

Accountability and Support Systems

Accountability and support systems can bolster the power of habits and routines. By sharing goals, progress, or challenges with others, individuals create external sources of motivation and feedback, increasing the likelihood of maintaining discipline.

Continuous Improvement and Adaptability

Cultivating discipline through habits and routines is an ongoing process that requires continuous improvement and adaptability. It involves reflecting on the effectiveness of current habits and routines, making adjustments as needed, and embracing a growth mindset to foster discipline over the long term.

Understanding the science behind habit formation and the benefits of effective routines provides individuals with powerful tools for cultivating discipline. By leveraging habit formation processes, identifying keystone habits, implementing effective routines, utilizing implementation intentions, and seeking accountability and support, individuals can establish a strong foundation for disciplined behavior. The power of habits and routines lies in their ability to automate disciplined actions, reduce reliance on willpower, and create an environment conducive to sustained discipline and success in various areas of life.

Delayed Gratification and the Marshmallow Experiment

The marshmallow experiment, conducted by psychologist Walter Mischel in the 1960s, is a well-known study that shed light on the concept of delayed gratification and its impact on discipline and long-term success. This comprehensive explanation describes the marshmallow experiment and its implications.

The Marshmallow Experiment

In the marshmallow experiment, young children were offered a choice between eating one marshmallow immediately or waiting for a short period to receive two marshmallows. The study aimed to examine the ability to delay gratification and the subsequent outcomes.

Delayed Gratification

Delayed gratification refers to the ability to resist immediate rewards in favor of larger, more desirable rewards in the future. It involves exercising self-control, willpower, and the ability to manage impulses.

Findings of the Marshmallow Experiment

The marshmallow experiment revealed that children who were able to delay gratification and wait for the second marshmallow exhibited better life outcomes later in life, including higher academic achievement, healthier lifestyle choices, and improved social skills.

Implications for Discipline

The marshmallow experiment highlights the importance of delayed gratification in fostering discipline. The ability to resist immediate temptations and stay focused on long-term goals is a crucial factor in maintaining discipline and achieving success.

Cognitive Strategies Employed

The children who were successful in delaying gratification employed various cognitive strategies. They used distraction techniques, such as looking away from the marshmallow, mentally reframed the situation, and focused on the long-term benefits of waiting.

Predictive Power of Delayed Gratification

Researchers have found that the ability to delay gratification during childhood predicts important life outcomes. Individuals who develop this skill are more likely to exhibit greater self-control, perseverance, and discipline in adolescence and adulthood, leading to increased success in various domains.

Enhancing Delayed Gratification

Delayed gratification is a skill that can be enhanced and developed over time. Individuals can strengthen their ability to delay gratification by practicing self-control in everyday situations, setting clear goals, visualizing long-term rewards, and implementing strategies to manage impulses.

Building Patience and Resilience

Delayed gratification fosters patience and resilience, as it requires individuals to tolerate short-term discomfort or sacrifice for the sake of long-term gains. This resilience strengthens discipline and provides individuals with the capacity to overcome challenges on the path to success.

Contextual Factors

The marshmallow experiment also highlighted the influence of contextual factors on delayed gratification. Factors such as trust in the experimenter, perceived reliability of the promised reward, and the child's individual circumstances can impact their decision to delay gratification.

Transferability to Real-Life Situations

The lessons learned from the marshmallow experiment are transferable to real-life situations. By understanding the importance of delayed gratification and cultivating the ability to resist immediate temptations, individuals can make disciplined choices, persevere through challenges, and work towards long-term success.

The marshmallow experiment provides valuable insights into the significance of delayed gratification in discipline and long-term success. It underscores the role of self-control, willpower, and the ability to manage impulses in maintaining discipline and achieving desired outcomes. By recognizing the power of delayed gratification and implementing strategies to enhance this skill, individuals can foster discipline, make informed choices, and work toward their long-term goals.

The Role of Motivation in Sustaining Discipline

Motivation plays a crucial role in sustaining discipline and achieving long-term success. This comprehensive explanation explores the relationship between motivation and discipline, differentiates between intrinsic and extrinsic motivation, and provides strategies for maintaining motivation during challenging times.

Motivation and Discipline

Motivation refers to the driving force that initiates, directs, and sustains behavior towards a goal. It acts as a catalyst for maintaining discipline by providing the energy and enthusiasm necessary to stay committed to one's objectives.

Intrinsic Motivation

Intrinsic motivation stems from internal factors, such as personal enjoyment, interest, and a sense of purpose. When individuals are intrinsically motivated, they engage in activities for the inherent satisfaction and fulfillment they derive from the task itself, which can bolster discipline.

Extrinsic Motivation

Extrinsic motivation arises from external factors, such as rewards, recognition, or punishments. While extrinsic motivation can initially spark discipline, it may not be as sustainable in the long term if the external incentives diminish. Balancing extrinsic motivators with intrinsic motivations is key to maintaining discipline.

Setting Meaningful Goals

Meaningful and personally relevant goals provide a strong foundation for motivation and discipline. By setting goals aligned with one's values, interests, and aspirations, individuals tap into their intrinsic motivation, increasing their commitment to disciplined action.

Cultivating a Growth Mindset

Adopting a growth mindset enhances motivation and discipline. Embracing the belief that abilities can be developed through effort and practice enables individuals to view challenges as opportunities for growth, maintaining their motivation even in the face of setbacks.

Creating a supportive environment

Surrounding oneself with a supportive environment can enhance motivation and discipline. Being in the company of like-minded individuals, seeking mentors or accountability partners, and having access to resources that foster growth and learning can help maintain motivation during challenging times.

Regular Progress Monitoring

Tracking progress towards goals is an effective strategy for maintaining motivation. Regularly monitoring and celebrating small milestones and accomplishments provides a sense of achievement and reinforces discipline by recognizing the progress made.

Self-Reflection and Self-Reward

Engaging in self-reflection allows individuals to identify their intrinsic motivations and connect with their deeper aspirations. Additionally, incorporating self-reward systems, such as treating oneself to a small indulgence after completing a task or achieving a milestone, can reinforce discipline and provide additional motivation.

Visualization and Affirmations

Visualization and affirmations can boost motivation by creating a mental image of desired outcomes and reinforcing positive beliefs about one's abilities. By visualizing success and reciting affirmations that align with discipline and perseverance, individuals can strengthen their motivation to stay on track.

Seeking Inspiration and Renewal

Engaging in activities that inspire and energize can help maintain motivation during challenging times. Seeking inspiration through books, podcasts, or connecting with individuals who have achieved similar goals can reignite motivation and provide the necessary boost to sustain discipline.

Understanding the relationship between motivation and discipline is key to sustaining long-term commitment to goals. By leveraging intrinsic motivation, setting meaningful goals, cultivating a growth mindset, creating a supportive environment, monitoring progress, engaging in self-reflection and self-reward, visualizing success, and seeking inspiration, individuals can sustain their motivation and foster discipline, even in the face of obstacles and difficulties. By continually nurturing motivation, individuals increase their likelihood of maintaining discipline and achieving their desired outcomes.

The Psychology of Goal Setting

Goal setting is a powerful psychological process that propels individuals towards desired outcomes. This comprehensive explanation explores the psychology behind effective goal setting, highlighting the importance of SMART goals.

Goal Setting and Motivation

Goals serve as a powerful source of motivation. By setting clear objectives, individuals create a target to strive for, igniting their intrinsic motivation and providing a sense of purpose and direction.

Specificity

Specific goals are more effective than vague ones. By clearly defining the desired outcome, individuals can direct their efforts and resources towards it, thereby enhancing the chances of success.

Measurability

Measurable goals enable individuals to track their progress and assess their level of achievement. The ability to measure progress provides a sense of accomplishment and facilitates the adjustment of strategies if necessary.

Achievability

Goals Goals should be challenging yet attainable. Setting overly ambitious goals that are beyond one's capabilities can lead to frustration and demotivation. It is essential to strike a balance between setting stretch goals and ensuring they are realistically achievable.

Relevance

Goals must align with an individual's values, interests, and aspirations. When goals are personally meaningful and relevant, individuals are more likely to remain committed, persevere through challenges, and maintain discipline to achieve them.

Time-Bound

Setting time-bound goals establishes a sense of urgency and creates a timeline for action. The presence of deadlines enhances motivation, prevents procrastination, and encourages disciplined behavior.

Self-Efficacy

Goal setting can enhance self-efficacy, which is an individual's belief in their ability to succeed. By setting challenging yet attainable goals and experiencing progress towards them, individuals develop a sense of competence and confidence, strengthening their belief in their ability to achieve future goals.

Feedback and Adjustment

Regular feedback on goal progress is important for maintaining motivation and adjusting strategies if necessary. Feedback provides individuals with valuable information about their performance, helps identify areas for improvement, and reinforces discipline.

Visualization and a Positive Mindset

Visualizing the achievement of goals and maintaining a positive mindset are powerful psychological techniques in goal setting. By creating vivid mental images of success and cultivating positive beliefs about one's abilities, individuals enhance motivation, maintain discipline, and overcome obstacles.

Commitment and Accountability

Making a public commitment to goals and establishing accountability systems increases the likelihood of maintaining discipline. Sharing goals with others, seeking support from mentors or accountability partners, and tracking progress collectively enhance motivation and discipline.

Understanding the psychology behind effective goal setting is instrumental in maximizing success. By setting specific, measurable, achievable, relevant, and time-bound goals, individuals harness the power of motivation, self-efficacy, and visualization. Additionally, regular feedback, commitment, and accountability contribute to sustained discipline and goal attainment. By incorporating these psychological principles into the goal-setting process, individuals can optimize their chances of success and cultivate a disciplined approach towards achieving their desired outcomes.

Self-Monitoring and Feedback

Self-monitoring and feedback are powerful tools that facilitate discipline and self-control. This comprehensive explanation reviews the role of self-monitoring and feedback in fostering discipline and outlines various techniques to enhance self-control and success.

Self-Monitoring

Self-monitoring involves observing and tracking one's thoughts, behaviors, and progress towards goals. By increasing self-awareness, individuals gain valuable insights into their patterns of behavior, allowing them to identify areas for improvement and make necessary adjustments.

Self-Reflection

Self-reflection is a technique that promotes deep introspection and analysis of one's thoughts, feelings, and actions. Engaging in regular self-reflection enables individuals to evaluate their level of discipline, identify obstacles or triggers, and develop strategies to overcome challenges.

Journaling

Journaling is a powerful self-monitoring tool that involves writing down thoughts, experiences, and reflections. By maintaining a journal, individuals can record their progress, track their emotions, and gain a better understanding of the factors that influence their discipline and self-control.

Goal Tracking

Tracking Tracking progress towards goals is an effective feedback mechanism. Whether through physical or digital means, regularly monitoring and recording progress provides individuals with a visual representation of their achievements, helping them stay motivated and disciplined.

Behavior Tracking

Tracking behaviors related to discipline and self-control helps individuals identify patterns, triggers, and areas for improvement. By monitoring behaviors such as procrastination, time management, or adherence to routines, individuals can gain insight into their habits and make conscious efforts to develop discipline.

Feedback Loops

Establishing feedback loops involves seeking feedback from trusted individuals or mentors who can provide objective perspectives. Feedback offers valuable insights, highlights blind spots, and suggests areas for growth, ultimately contributing to enhanced discipline and self-control.

Self-Reward Systems

Incorporating self-reward systems into self-monitoring and feedback processes can reinforce discipline and motivation. Setting up a system where individuals reward themselves for meeting specific milestones or exhibiting disciplined behavior provides positive reinforcement and encourages continued effort.

Reflection Prompts

Using reflection prompts can guide individuals in their self-monitoring and feedback process. Questions such as "What worked well today?" "What could I have done differently?" or "What obstacles did I encounter? prompt individuals to critically evaluate their actions, fostering self-awareness and discipline.

Data Analysis

Analyzing data collected through self-monitoring techniques allows individuals to identify trends and patterns. By analyzing trends, individuals can make informed decisions, adjust strategies, and leverage insights to enhance their self-control and discipline.

Continuous Improvement

We should view self-monitoring and feedback as a continuous improvement process. Regularly reviewing progress, reflecting on experiences, and adjusting approaches based on feedback and insights contribute to the development of discipline and the achievement of long-term success.

Incorporating self-monitoring and feedback techniques such as self-reflection, journaling, goal tracking, and seeking feedback enhances self-control and discipline. These practices increase self-awareness, provide valuable insights, and enable individuals to make informed decisions and adjustments. By embracing self-monitoring and feedback as integral components of the discipline journey, individuals can cultivate greater self-control, maintain motivation, and ultimately achieve their goals and aspirations.

Cognitive Strategies for Enhancing Self-Control

Cognitive strategies play a significant role in enhancing self-control and fostering discipline. This comprehensive explanation explores cognitive strategies, including cognitive restructuring and attentional control, and how they can strengthen self-control in different contexts.

Cognitive Restructuring

Cognitive restructuring involves identifying and challenging negative or unhelpful thoughts and replacing them with more rational and constructive ones. By reframing thoughts and beliefs that undermine discipline, individuals can develop a more positive and supportive mindset, enhancing self-control.

Self-Awareness

Developing self-awareness is a fundamental cognitive strategy for enhancing self-control. By recognizing one's thoughts, emotions, and triggers that lead to undisciplined behavior, individuals can proactively intervene and implement strategies to regain control.

Thought Stopping

Thought stopping is a technique that involves consciously interrupting and redirecting intrusive or distracting thoughts. By using cues or verbal commands to halt unhelpful thoughts, individuals can redirect their attention towards more disciplined and productive activities.

Attentional Control

Attentional control refers to the ability to focus and sustain attention on relevant tasks while filtering out distractions. By practicing attentional control techniques, such as mindfulness or meditation, individuals can strengthen their ability to resist temptations, maintain focus, and sustain discipline.

Implementation Intentions

Implementation intentions involve formulating specific plans that outline when, where, and how to act in order to achieve a goal. By clearly defining the desired actions and anticipating potential obstacles, individuals can overcome self-control challenges and stay disciplined.

Delayed Gratification

Delayed gratification is a cognitive strategy that involves resisting immediate rewards in favor of long-term benefits. By training oneself to delay gratification, individuals strengthen their self-control, develop patience, and make choices aligned with their long-term goals.

Cognitive Load Management

Cognitive load refers to the mental effort required to process information and make decisions. Managing cognitive load involves simplifying tasks, breaking them down into smaller steps, and reducing distractions, enabling individuals to conserve mental resources and maintain self-control.

Response inhibition

Response inhibition is the ability to suppress impulsive or automatic responses. By practicing response inhibition, individuals can resist immediate gratification or impulsive actions that undermine discipline, allowing for more thoughtful and controlled behavior.

Self-Talk

Engaging in positive and self-encouraging self-talk can strengthen self-control. By using affirmations, self-reminders, or motivational statements, individuals can boost their self-confidence, reinforce discipline, and overcome self-control challenges.

Goal Priming

Goal priming involves consciously activating goals through cues or reminders. By exposing oneself to visual or verbal cues associated with goals, individuals can heighten their motivation, direct their attention towards disciplined actions, and maintain focus on achieving desired outcomes.

Cognitive strategies such as cognitive restructuring, attentional control, implementation intentions, and delayed gratification can significantly enhance self-control and support discipline in various contexts. By adopting these strategies, individuals can manage their thoughts, focus their attention, resist temptations, and make deliberate choices aligned with their long-term goals. Building cognitive resilience and utilizing these strategies empowers individuals to overcome challenges, maintain discipline, and achieve greater success in their endeavors.

Building Resilience and Overcoming Setbacks

Resilience is a crucial psychological trait that enables individuals to navigate setbacks, challenges, and adversities while maintaining discipline and focus on their long-term success. This comprehensive explanation explores the psychological aspects of resilience and provides strategies for building it and overcoming setbacks.

Understanding Resilience

Resilience refers to the ability to bounce back from setbacks, adapt to change, and thrive in the face of adversity. It involves maintaining a positive mindset, effectively coping with stress, and persevering through challenges while staying committed to one's goals.

Positive Reframing

Positive reframing involves shifting one's perspective on setbacks and challenges. By viewing setbacks as opportunities for growth and learning, individuals can maintain a positive mindset, retain discipline, and identify innovative solutions to overcome obstacles.

Emotional Regulation

Building resilience requires effective emotional regulation. By developing emotional intelligence and cultivating strategies for managing stress, individuals can maintain composure, make rational decisions, and preserve discipline during challenging times.

Social Support

Seeking and utilizing social support networks is crucial in building resilience. Connecting with others who provide emotional support, guidance, and encouragement can help individuals stay focused, motivated, and disciplined in the face of setbacks.

Self-Care

Prioritizing self-care is essential for building resilience. Engaging in activities that promote physical and mental well-being, such as exercise, adequate sleep, and mindfulness, enhances one's ability to handle setbacks, maintain discipline, and sustain focus on long-term success.

Cognitive Flexibility

Developing cognitive flexibility allows individuals to adapt to changing circumstances and adjust their strategies accordingly. By embracing new perspectives, generating alternative solutions, and remaining open to different approaches, individuals can navigate setbacks with resilience and maintain discipline.

Learning from Setbacks

Embracing setbacks as learning opportunities is crucial for building resilience. Reflecting on setbacks, identifying lessons learned, and applying those lessons to future endeavors fosters personal growth, strengthens discipline, and fuels ongoing motivation.

Goal Adjustment

Building resilience involves the willingness to adjust goals when necessary. By recognizing when goals are no longer feasible or require modification, individuals can adapt their plans, maintain discipline, and channel their efforts towards new pathways for success.

Building Self-Efficacy

Self-efficacy, the belief in one's ability to succeed, is a key component of resilience. By setting achievable goals, experiencing small successes, and celebrating milestones, individuals can strengthen their self-efficacy, bolster discipline, and persevere through setbacks.

Maintaining a Long-Term Perspective

Maintaining a long-term outlook and remaining committed to the ultimate goal of success is crucial when faced with setbacks. Keeping sight of long-term goals helps individuals navigate temporary setbacks, maintain discipline, and stay motivated to continue their journey.

Building resilience and overcoming setbacks requires a combination of psychological strategies and self-care practices. By adopting a positive mindset, seeking social support, practicing emotional regulation, and staying focused on long-term goals, individuals can cultivate resilience, bounce back from setbacks, and maintain discipline in pursuit of their aspirations. Embracing setbacks as opportunities for growth, learning, and adaptation enables individuals to develop the resilience necessary to overcome challenges and ultimately achieve long-term success.

Chapter 3

Nurturing Discipline

Building Habits that Foster Self-Control and Drive

Understanding the Power of Habits

Habits have a major influence on our behavior and daily routines. They are automatic patterns of behavior that we engage in without much conscious thought. Understanding the power of habits is essential in cultivating discipline and self-control. Here, we will explore the role of habits and how they contribute to discipline and self-control.

Habit Formation

Habits are formed through repetition and reinforcement. When we consistently perform a behavior in a specific context, it becomes ingrained in our neural pathways and becomes a habit. Understanding the process of habit formation helps us recognize the steps needed to cultivate disciplined habits.

Habit Loops

Habits are built around a loop consisting of three elements: cue, routine, and reward. The cue triggers the behavior, the routine is the behavior itself, and the reward reinforces the habit. By understanding this loop, we can identify cues and rewards associated with undisciplined behaviors and replace them with more productive alternatives.

Automatic Behavior

Habits function automatically, circumventing the need for conscious decision-making processes. This allows us to conserve mental energy and make it easier to engage in disciplined behaviors consistently. By harnessing the power of habits, we can rely less on willpower and make disciplined choices effortlessly.

Habit Triggers

Habits are often triggered by specific cues or stimuli in our environment. These triggers prompt the automatic execution of the associated behavior. By identifying the triggers that lead to undisciplined behaviors, we can modify our environment and create triggers that support disciplined actions.

Habits and Self-Control

Habits play a crucial role in supporting self-control and discipline. When disciplined actions become habitual, we are less likely to succumb to short-term impulses or make impulsive decisions. Habits provide a structure that guides our behavior and allows us to stay on track towards our goals.

Habit Substitution

To develop discipline, it can be advantageous to substitute undisciplined habits with more productive ones. By consciously replacing undesirable habits with disciplined behaviors, we create a positive shift in our daily routines and promote self-control.

Habit Consistency

Consistency is key in building disciplined habits. By consistently performing disciplined behaviors, they become reinforced and easier to maintain over time. Establishing a routine and committing to it helps solidify disciplined habits and strengthens self-control.

Habit and Goal Alignment

Habits can align with our long-term goals and contribute to their achievement. By identifying the habits that support our desired outcomes, we can intentionally develop and reinforce those habits to stay disciplined and make progress towards our goals.

Habit Cues and Environment

Our environment plays a significant role in habit formation and maintenance. By creating an environment that supports disciplined behaviors and removing or modifying cues that trigger undisciplined actions, we can shape our environment to facilitate self-control and discipline.

Habit Reflection and Adjustment

Regularly reflecting on our habits allows us to assess their effectiveness and make adjustments as needed. By evaluating the impact of our habits on our discipline and self-control, we can refine and optimize them to better align with our goals.

Understanding the power of habits is instrumental in cultivating discipline and self-control. By recognizing the role of habits in shaping our behavior, harnessing the habit loop, aligning habits with our goals, and creating supportive environments, we can build disciplined habits that contribute to our long-term success. Embracing the power of habits empowers us to make positive changes and maintain the discipline needed to achieve our aspirations.

Habit Formation

Habits are automatic behaviors that we perform regularly and effortlessly. Understanding the science behind habit formation is essential for creating lasting habits that contribute to discipline and self-control. Here, we will explore the process of habit formation and the key factors involved.

Cue

Habits begin with a cue, which is a trigger that prompts the behavior. Cues can be external (such as a specific time of day or a visual stimulus) or internal (such as an emotional state or a thought). Identifying the cues that precede a habit is crucial in understanding and modifying the behavior.

Routine

The routine is the behavior itself—the action we take in response to the cue. This is the core component of the habit. Repetition of the routine strengthens the neural pathways associated with the habit and makes it more automatic over time.

Reward

The reward is the positive reinforcement that follows the behavior. It satisfies a need or provides a sense of pleasure, which reinforces the habit loop. Rewards can be tangible (such as a treat) or intrinsic (such as a sense of accomplishment).

Dopamine

Dopamine, a neurotransmitter in the brain, plays a significant role in habit formation. It is released during the reward phase and creates a pleasurable sensation, motivating us to repeat the behavior. Dopamine reinforces the habit loop and strengthens the neural connections associated with it.

Repetition

Repetition is key to habit formation. Consistently engaging in the behavior strengthens the neural pathways and makes the habit more automatic. Research suggests that it takes an average of 66 days for a behavior to become a habit, although this duration can vary depending on the complexity of the habit and individual differences.

Context-Dependent

Habits are context-dependent, meaning they are often triggered by specific environments, situations, or cues. Understanding the context in which habits occur allows us to modify our environment and create cues that support disciplined behaviors.

Habit Stacking

Habit stacking involves attaching a new habit to an existing one. By linking a desired behavior to an established habit, we leverage the existing neural pathways and make it easier to adopt the new behavior. Habit stacking is a powerful technique for creating lasting habits.

Belief and Identity

Belief and identity play a role in habit formation. When we believe that we are capable of change and identify ourselves as someone who possesses disciplined habits, we are more likely to adopt and maintain them. Cultivating a growth mindset and aligning our self-image with disciplined behavior can enhance habit formation.

Environment and Social Influence

Our environment and social context can influence habit formation. Surrounding ourselves with supportive environments and like-minded individuals who exhibit disciplined habits can enhance our habit formation. Social accountability and support can also play a crucial role in sustaining habits.

Habit Modification

Modifying existing habits or replacing undisciplined habits with more desirable ones is possible through intentional effort. By recognizing the cues and rewards associated with undesired habits and consciously choosing alternative routines, we can reshape our habits and foster discipline.

Understanding the science behind habit formation empowers us to create lasting habits that support discipline and self-control. By recognizing the role of cues, routines, and rewards, leveraging the power of dopamine, embracing repetition, and considering the context and social influences, we can intentionally shape our habits for positive change. Building lasting habits requires commitment, consistency, and an understanding of the underlying mechanisms at play. With knowledge and deliberate practice, we can cultivate disciplined habits that contribute to our personal growth and success.

The Habit Loop

The habit loop is a fundamental concept in understanding and shaping our habits. It consists of three components: cue, routine, and reward. By understanding how these elements interact, we can leverage the habit loop to build disciplined habits. Here's a comprehensive explanation of the habit loop and its application in cultivating discipline.

Cue

The cue is the trigger that prompts the habit. It can be a specific time of day, location, emotional state, or even another action. Cues create a link between our environment or internal state and the behavior we want to engage in. Recognizing the cues that precede our desired disciplined habits allows us to intentionally create the conditions for their activation.

Routine

The routine is the behavior itself—the action we take in response to the cue. It is the core component of the habit loop. The routine can be a physical action, a mental process, or an emotional response. Engaging in the desired routine consistently strengthens the neural pathways associated with the habit and makes it more automatic over time.

Reward

The reward is the positive reinforcement that follows the behavior. It satisfies a need or provides a sense of pleasure. Rewards can be tangible, such as a treat or a feeling of accomplishment, or intrinsic, such as a sense of satisfaction. The reward is what motivates us to repeat the behavior and reinforces the habit loop.

Craving

Craving is an additional element that is sometimes included in the habit loop. It refers to the anticipation or desire for the reward. Cravings drive our motivation to engage in the routine and complete the habit loop. By understanding our cravings and what we truly desire from the habit, we can better design the habit loop for success.

Leveraging Habit Loop

To build disciplined habits, we can leverage the habit loop by deliberately manipulating its components. By identifying the cues that trigger undisciplined behaviors, we can modify or replace them with cues that prompt disciplined actions. Likewise, we can design routines that align with our desired disciplined behaviors and choose rewards that reinforce them.

Cue Awareness

Increasing our awareness of the cues that trigger our habits is key to leveraging the habit loop. By consciously recognizing the cues, we can interrupt the automatic response and make a deliberate choice to engage in the disciplined routine instead. Mindfulness and self-reflection can enhance cue awareness.

Routine Design

Designing effective routines is essential for building disciplined habits. The routine should be specific, actionable, and aligned with our goals. Breaking the routine down into smaller steps and making it manageable increases the likelihood of success and reduces resistance.

Reward Optimization

Choosing rewards that are meaningful and aligned with our values and goals strengthens the habit loop. Rewards should be enjoyable and provide a sense of satisfaction. It can be helpful to experiment with different rewards and find what truly motivates and reinforces the desired behavior.

Habit Tracking

Tracking our habits and monitoring our progress allows us to observe the habit loop in action. By keeping a habit journal, using habit tracking apps, or creating visual cues, we can reinforce our commitment to disciplined habits and celebrate our achievements along the way.

Habit Consistency

Consistency is crucial for habit formation and discipline. Engaging in the routine consistently, even on days when motivation is low, reinforces the habit loop and strengthens the neural connections associated with the disciplined behavior. Embracing a growth mindset and viewing occasional setbacks as learning opportunities can help maintain consistency.

Understanding and leveraging the habit loop empowers us to build disciplined habits that support our goals. By identifying cues, designing effective routines, optimizing rewards, and tracking our progress, we can shape the habit loop in our favor. Building disciplined habits requires patience, practice, and self-awareness. With time and commitment, we can harness the power of the habit loop to cultivate discipline and drive our personal growth and success.

Habit Stacking

Habit stacking is a powerful technique that can help us reinforce discipline and establish new habits. It involves attaching new habits to existing ones by leveraging the power of associations and routines. By capitalizing on our existing habits, we can create a strong routine that supports our disciplined behaviors. Here's a comprehensive explanation of habit stacking and its application in cultivating discipline.

Leveraging Existing Habits

Habit stacking works by piggybacking new habits onto existing ones. We identify a habit that we already perform consistently and use it as a cue or trigger for the new habit we want to develop. By linking the new behavior to an existing one, we take advantage of the automaticity and familiarity of the established habit.

Creating Associations

When we attach a new habit to an existing one, we create a mental association between the two. This association helps trigger the desired behavior and makes it easier to remember and perform. Over time, the new habit becomes intertwined with the existing one, forming a strong routine.

Simplifying Behavior Change

Habit stacking simplifies the process of behavior change. Instead of relying solely on willpower or motivation to initiate a new habit, we utilize the momentum and reliability of an existing habit to kickstart the desired behavior. This strategy makes it more likely for the new habit to stick and reduces the resistance to change.

Identifying Cue-Action Pairs

To effectively habit stack, we need to identify cue-action pairs. The cue is the existing habit that will serve as the trigger, and the action is the new habit we want to establish. For example, if we have a habit of brushing our teeth every morning, we can stack a new habit of doing a short meditation immediately after brushing.

Specificity and Clarity

When engaging in habit stacking, it is crucial to be specific and clear about the new habit that we wish to incorporate. The action should be well-defined and actionable. By specifying the exact behavior we want to engage in, we eliminate ambiguity and increase the chances of successful habit formation.

BuildingMomentum

Habit stacking allows us to build momentum by capitalizing on the habits we already have in place. As we consistently perform the existing habit and follow it immediately with the new habit, we create a positive momentum that reinforces both behaviors. This process helps maintain consistency and overcome resistance.

Habit Stacking Chains

Habit stacking can create chains of habits, where each one triggers the next. This helps establish a comprehensive routine that supports discipline and maximizes productivity. By linking multiple habits together, we create a powerful structure that facilitates goal attainment.

Flexibility and Adaptability

Habit stacking is flexible and adaptable to different contexts and lifestyles. We can customize our habit stacks based on our unique goals and preferences. It allows for creativity and experimentation, enabling us to find combinations that work best for us.

Mindful Implementation

While habit stacking can be a useful tool, it's important to be mindful of the habits we choose to stack. We should ensure that the existing habit aligns with our values and the new habit contributes to our overall well-being and growth. Mindful implementation ensures that we create supportive routines that lead to long-term success.

Reinforcing Discipline

Habit stacking reinforces discipline by providing structure and consistency. By adhering to a routine of stacked habits, we train ourselves to be more disciplined and intentional in our actions. The cumulative effect of consistent habits strengthens self-control and fosters discipline in various aspects of our lives.

Habit stacking is a practical and effective strategy for reinforcing discipline and building new habits. By harnessing the power of existing routines, creating associations, and being mindful in our implementation, we can establish a strong foundation for disciplined behavior and drive our personal and professional success.

Habit Tracking

Habit tracking is a valuable practice that can greatly support our efforts to cultivate discipline and establish new habits. By monitoring and measuring our progress, we gain insights into our behavior patterns, stay accountable, and make informed adjustments. Here's a comprehensive explanation of habit tracking, its significance, and the different methods used to track and measure habits:

Increased Self-Awareness

Habit tracking enhances self-awareness by bringing our attention to our daily behaviors. It allows us to observe patterns, identify triggers, and recognize areas where discipline may be lacking. By becoming more aware of our habits, we gain valuable insights that can guide our efforts towards positive change.

Accountability and Motivation

Tracking our habits holds us accountable to ourselves. When we record our daily actions, we have a visual representation of our progress, which can serve as a powerful motivator. Seeing our successes and areas for improvement reinforces our commitment to discipline and encourages us to stay on track.

Measurement and Progress Evaluation

Habit tracking enables us to measure our progress over time. By consistently recording our habits, we can analyze trends, identify growth areas, and assess our overall improvement. It provides a tangible way to evaluate our efforts and celebrate milestones along the journey to discipline.

Habit Trackers

Habit trackers are tools specifically designed to monitor and visualize our habits. They often come in the form of charts or grids where we can mark our daily progress. Habit trackers provide a visual representation of our habits, making it easier to track and assess our consistency.

Habit-Tracking Apps

In the digital age, habit-tracking apps offer convenience and flexibility. These apps provide a range of features, such as customizable habit lists, reminders, and progress charts. They allow us to track habits on our smartphones, making it accessible and easy to record our daily actions on the go.

Habit Journals

Habit journals offer a more personal and reflective approach to habit tracking. They provide space to write about our experiences, emotions, and reflections related to our habits. Habit journals allow us to explore the reasons behind our actions, fostering self-discovery and facilitating meaningful behavior change.

Choosing Right Method

The choice of a habit-tracking method depends on personal preferences and lifestyle. Some individuals may prefer the simplicity and visual appeal of habit trackers, while others may find the reflective nature of habit journals more beneficial. Experimenting with different methods can help determine the most effective approach for tracking habits.

Setting Specific Metrics

When tracking habits, it's essential to define specific metrics for measurement. Such activities could include tracking the frequency, duration, or quality of the habit. By setting clear metrics, we can objectively assess our progress and determine whether adjustments are necessary.

Tracking Habit Triggers

Habit tracking can go beyond merely recording the habit itself. It can also involve tracking the triggers that precede the habit. Identifying and monitoring triggers can help us better understand the circumstances that prompt our actions, allowing us to modify our environment or routines to support discipline.

Reflecting on Progress

Regular reflection on our progress should accompany habit tracking. Taking the time to review our habits and evaluate our efforts provides valuable feedback for growth. Reflective practices, such as reviewing habit logs or conducting self-assessments, help us gain insights, learn from our experiences, and refine our approach to discipline.

Habit tracking is a powerful tool for fostering discipline and creating positive change. By increasing self-awareness, staying accountable, and measuring our progress through habit trackers, apps, journals, or other methods, we can effectively monitor our habits, make adjustments as needed, and ultimately cultivate discipline for long-term success.

Habit Triggers and Cues

Habit triggers and cues play a crucial role in the formation and maintenance of disciplined habits. These cues serve as reminders and signals that prompt us to engage in specific behaviors automatically and without conscious effort. Understanding the role of triggers and cues can help us design environments that support disciplined habits. Here's a comprehensive explanation of habit triggers and cues, as well as their significance in habit formation.

Definition of Triggers and Cues

Triggers and cues are stimuli that precede and initiate habitual behaviors. They can be external, such as specific objects or environmental cues, or internal, such as emotions or thoughts. Triggers and cues act as signals to our brain, signaling that it's time to perform a particular habit.

Associative Learning

The formation of habits relies on associative learning, where our brain connects the habit with a specific trigger or cue. Through repeated exposure and reinforcement, the association becomes stronger, making the behavior more automatic and less dependent on conscious decision-making.

Identifying Existing Triggers

To leverage triggers effectively, it's important to identify the existing cues that prompt our desired habits. The procedure requires observation and self-awareness to recognize the patterns and circumstances that typically precede the habit. By pinpointing these triggers, we can intentionally design our environment to support disciplined behaviors.

Designing Intentional Cues

We can intentionally design cues that elicit our desired habits in addition to recognizing the triggers that are already there. This involves consciously designing our environment or routine to include visual, auditory, or sensory cues that serve as reminders. For example, placing a water bottle on our desk can serve as a cue to drink more water throughout the day.

Habit-Stacking as a Cue Strategy

Habit stacking, as mentioned earlier, is a powerful technique that leverages existing habits as triggers for new habits. By attaching a new habit to an existing one, we utilize the natural cue of the established habit to prompt the desired behavior. This strategy capitalizes on the power of associations to support disciplined habits.

Environmental Cues

Our physical environment can be a powerful source of cues that influence our habits. By strategically arranging our surroundings, we can create cues that remind us to engage in disciplined behaviors. One way to encourage morning exercise is to place your workout attire close to your bed.

Time-Based Cues

Time-based cues rely on certain times of the day or specific moments in our routine to trigger habits. These cues can be linked to events such as meals, breaks, or transitions between activities. By aligning our habits with these time-based cues, we can establish a consistent routine and reinforce discipline.

Emotional Cues

Emotions can act as triggers for certain habits. We may engage in certain behaviors as a response to specific emotions, whether it's stress, boredom, or happiness. Being mindful of our emotional states and recognizing the habits associated with them allows us to proactively manage our responses and choose more disciplined behaviors.

Anchoring Cues

Anchoring cues involve associating a desired habit with an existing or recurring event. For instance, we can use the act of sitting down at our desk as a cue to initiate a concentrated work session. Anchoring cues create a strong link between the trigger event and the desired behavior, facilitating habit formation.

Consistency and Repetition

The effectiveness of triggers and cues relies on consistency and repetition. The more consistently we associate a cue with a habit and repeat the behavior, the stronger the association becomes. By intentionally repeating the desired behavior in response to the trigger, we reinforce the habit and make it more automatic.

Knowing how cues and triggers contribute to the development of habits allows us to deliberately create settings that encourage healthy routines. Identifying existing triggers, creating intentional cues, leveraging habit stacking, and utilizing various cue strategies enable us to establish disciplined behaviors more effectively. By aligning our environments and routines with our desired habits, we set ourselves up for success in cultivating discipline and achieving our goals.

Habit Reinforcement

Reinforcing disciplined habits is essential for their long-term sustainability and effectiveness. By implementing effective reinforcement techniques, we can increase the likelihood of consistently engaging in desired behaviors and maintaining discipline. Here's a comprehensive explanation of habit reinforcement techniques and their significance in supporting disciplined habits.

Positive Reinforcement

Positive reinforcement involves rewarding ourselves for engaging in disciplined habits. It can be as simple as acknowledging and celebrating our accomplishments, treating ourselves to something enjoyable, or giving ourselves praise and encouragement. Positive reinforcement enhances motivation, strengthens the habit loop, and makes disciplined behaviors more enjoyable and satisfying.

Habit Tracking and Progress Monitoring

Habit tracking, as discussed earlier, serves as a form of reinforcement by providing a visual representation of our progress. Regularly reviewing our habit-tracking records and seeing the positive changes we've made can be highly motivating. It reinforces our commitment to discipline and encourages us to continue striving for improvement.

Accountability Systems

Establishing accountability systems can be a powerful tool for reinforcing disciplined habits. Such activities can involve partnering with an accountability buddy or joining a support group where members hold each other responsible for their habits. Accountability systems create a sense of responsibility, provide feedback and support, and increase the likelihood of following through with disciplined behaviors.

Habit Contracts

Habit contracts are written agreements we make with ourselves or others to reinforce disciplined habits. These contracts outline the specific habit, the desired frequency or duration, and the consequences for not following through. By formalizing our commitment and holding ourselves accountable to the terms of the contract, we reinforce discipline and create a sense of responsibility.

Visual Cues and Reminders

Visual cues and reminders serve as constant reinforcement for disciplined habits. These can include sticky notes, posters, or digital reminders that prompt us to engage in the desired behavior. Visual cues act as constant reminders of our goals, making it easier to maintain discipline and resist temptations.

Social Support

Social support plays a significant role in habit reinforcement. Sharing our goals and progress with supportive friends, family, or communities creates a positive social environment that encourages disciplined behaviors. Supportive individuals can provide motivation, offer guidance, and celebrate our successes, reinforcing our commitment to discipline.

Habit Celebrations

Celebrating milestones and achievements along the habit journey is a powerful form of reinforcement. By acknowledging our progress and rewarding ourselves for reaching milestones, we associate disciplined habits with positive experiences. Celebrations can be small or large, depending on the significance of the accomplishment, and can include treating ourselves to something special or engaging in a rewarding activity.

Self-Reflection and Self-Reward

Self-reflection allows us to assess our efforts, recognize our growth, and reinforce disciplined habits. By reflecting on the positive impact of our habits on our well-being, productivity, or personal growth, we reinforce their value and motivate ourselves to continue practicing them. Additionally, rewarding ourselves with self-care activities or personal treats can further reinforce our commitment to discipline.

Gamification

Gamification involves adding elements of competition, challenges, or rewards to our habit-building process. By turning disciplined habits into a game, we make them more engaging and enjoyable. The process can include setting up rewards or challenges for achieving certain milestones or using habit-tracking apps that incorporate gamified features.

Continuous Learning and Improvement

Continuous learning and improvement serve as intrinsic reinforcement for disciplined habits. By seeking knowledge, staying curious, and exploring new ways to refine our habits, we keep the habit loop active and reinforce our commitment to discipline. Learning about the benefits of disciplined behaviors and understanding the positive impact they have on our lives strengthens our motivation to maintain and improve them.

Implementing reinforcement techniques, such as positive reinforcement, accountability systems, social support, visual cues, celebrations, and continuous learning, enhances the effectiveness and sustainability of disciplined habits. These techniques provide the motivation, support, and reinforcement needed to maintain discipline and achieve long-term success.

Habit Resilience

Building disciplined habits is not always a linear process. There are challenges and setbacks that can hinder our progress and test our discipline. However, developing habit resilience is crucial in overcoming these obstacles and maintaining consistency in our behaviors. Here's a comprehensive explanation of habit resilience, including an understanding of the challenges that may arise and strategies to overcome setbacks.

Understanding Common Challenges

It's important to recognize the common challenges that may arise when building disciplined habits. These can include lack of motivation, distractions, external pressures, time constraints, fatigue, or unexpected events that disrupt our routines. By understanding these challenges, we can proactively prepare for them and develop strategies to address them.

Cultivating Self-Awareness

Self-awareness is key to habit resilience. By being aware of our strengths, weaknesses, triggers, and patterns, we can better anticipate challenges and develop strategies to overcome them. Regular self-reflection and mindfulness practices help us identify potential pitfalls and make conscious choices aligned with our disciplined habits.

Embracing Growth Mindset

Adopting a growth mindset is crucial in building habit resilience. Seeing setbacks and challenges as opportunities for growth rather than failures allows us to learn from them and adjust our approach. Embracing the belief that we can improve and overcome obstacles reinforces our determination to maintain discipline and bounce back from setbacks.

Flexibility and Adaptability

Being flexible and adaptable in our approach to disciplined habits is important. Life is full of unexpected circumstances, and it's necessary to adjust our routines and strategies accordingly. Embracing flexibility allows us to navigate challenges without losing sight of our long-term goals and commitment to discipline.

Developing Coping Strategies

Developing effective coping strategies is essential for habit resilience. These strategies can include stress management techniques, such as deep breathing or meditation, that help us navigate challenging situations without compromising our disciplined habits. Finding healthy ways to cope with stress, boredom, or emotional triggers strengthens our resilience and prevents derailing our progress.

Planning for Obstacles

Anticipating potential obstacles and creating contingency plans is a valuable habit and resilience strategy. By identifying the obstacles that may arise and developing alternative courses of action, we are better prepared to stay on track. For example, if our regular exercise routine is disrupted, having a backup plan, such as a home workout or outdoor activity, ensures that we don't abandon our disciplined habit completely.

Social Support and Accountability

Surrounding ourselves with supportive individuals who share similar goals and values can greatly enhance habit resilience. Engaging in communities and accountability groups or finding an accountability partner fosters motivation, encouragement, and a sense of accountability. Sharing our challenges, progress, and victories with others provides support during setbacks and helps maintain consistency.

Learning from Setbacks

Setbacks are opportunities for learning and growth. When we encounter obstacles or temporarily veer off track, it's important to reflect on the reasons behind the setback and extract valuable lessons from the experience. By learning from setbacks, we can adjust our strategies, strengthen our discipline, and prevent similar challenges in the future.

Revisiting Motivations and Goals

Periodically revisiting our motivations and goals helps reignite our passion for disciplined habits. It's normal for motivation to fluctuate over time, so reminding ourselves of the reasons we started and the benefits we seek reinforces our commitment. By reconnecting with our intrinsic motivations, we can overcome setbacks and maintain discipline.

Persistence and Self-Compassion

Building habit resilience requires persistence and self-compassion. It's essential to approach setbacks with kindness and understanding, recognizing that they are part of the journey. Persevering through challenges and being patient with ourselves allows us to bounce back stronger and continue working towards our disciplined habits.

By understanding the challenges, cultivating self-awareness, embracing a growth mindset, being flexible, developing coping strategies, planning for obstacles, seeking social support, learning from setbacks, revisiting motivations and goals, and practicing persistence and self-compassion, we can enhance our habit resilience and maintain consistency in disciplined habits.

Keystone Habits

Keystones are powerful habits that act as catalysts for positive change in various aspects of our lives. They are foundational behaviors that have a ripple effect, leading to the development of other productive habits and positively influencing different areas of life. Understanding the concept of keystone habits and how to identify and cultivate them can significantly enhance discipline. Here's a comprehensive explanation.

Definition of Keystone Habits

Keystone habits are key behaviors that have a disproportionate impact on other areas of our lives. They serve as a foundation for building discipline and creating a domino effect of positive change. These habits often create a ripple effect, influencing other behaviors and aspects of our lives.

Identifying Keystone Habits

Keystone habits can vary from person to person, but they generally fall into certain categories, such as health and fitness, mindfulness and self-care, organization and productivity, or personal relationships. To identify keystone habits, it's essential to reflect on behaviors that, when consistently practiced, have the greatest positive impact on other areas of life.

Examples of Keystone Habits

Examples of keystone habits include regular exercise, daily meditation or mindfulness practice, setting and reviewing goals, consistent sleep routines, maintaining a clean and organized environment, practicing gratitude, or developing effective communication skills. These habits often have a transformative influence on other habits and areas of life.

Ripple Effect of Keystone Habits

Keystone habits create a ripple effect by triggering a series of positive changes in various aspects of life. For example, regular exercise not only improves physical health but also boosts energy levels, enhances mental clarity, promotes better sleep, and increases self-discipline, which can spill over into other areas such as work productivity and personal relationships.

Cultivating Keystone Habits

Cultivating keystone habits requires consistency, commitment, and a focus on incremental progress. Start by selecting one or two keystone habits that align with your goals and values. Break them down into manageable steps and integrate them into your daily routine. Over time, as these habits become ingrained, they will naturally influence other behaviors and promote discipline in different areas of life.

Supporting Keystone Habits with Systems and Cues

Creating systems and implementing cues can reinforce keystone habits. For instance, if daily meditation is your keystone habit, you can establish a designated meditation space, set a specific time each day, and use reminders or meditation apps to support consistency. These external cues and structures can help make the habit more automatic and easier to maintain.

Tracking Progress and Celebrating Milestones

Monitoring your progress and celebrating milestones is essential when cultivating keystone habits. Keep track of your adherence to the habit and note any positive changes or improvements you observe in other areas of life. Celebrating milestones reinforces the value of the habit and provides motivation to continue practicing it.

Leveraging Keystone Habits during Challenging Times

Keystone habits can serve as anchors during challenging periods or when motivation is low. When faced with obstacles or setbacks, rely on your keystone habits to maintain discipline and stability. They can provide a sense of grounding and resilience, helping you stay on track even when circumstances are difficult.

Integrating Keystone Habits with Complementary Habits

Complementary habits are behaviors that support and reinforce keystone habits. Identify habits that align with and complement your keystone habits. For example, if regular exercise is your keystone habit, complementary habits could include meal planning, staying hydrated, or prioritizing rest and recovery.

Sustaining Keystone Habits for Long-Term Discipline

Sustaining keystone habits requires ongoing commitment and periodic reassessment. Continuously evaluate the effectiveness of your keystone habits and make adjustments as needed. As you cultivate discipline through keystone habits, be open to exploring new areas for growth and identifying additional keystone habits that can further enhance your overall well-being and success.

By recognizing the power of keystone habits, identifying them, cultivating them with consistency and intention, and leveraging their ripple effect on other areas of life, we can significantly enhance discipline and create positive, lasting change in our lives.

Habit Evolution

Habits play a crucial role in our lives, shaping our behaviors and influencing our outcomes. However, as circumstances change and we grow as individuals, it is necessary to acknowledge the importance of habit evolution. Habit evolution refers to the ongoing process of refining and adapting our habits to align with our changing goals, priorities, and environments. Here's a comprehensive explanation of the concept.

Understanding Habit Evolution

Habit evolution recognizes that habits are not fixed entities but should be flexible and adaptable. It involves a continuous process of assessing, adjusting, and refining our habits to ensure they remain relevant and effective in supporting our goals and maintaining discipline.

Recognizing Changing Circumstances

Life is dynamic, and circumstances are subject to change. New responsibilities, challenges, and opportunities may arise, requiring us to reassess our habits. By staying aware of our evolving circumstances, we can identify areas where our habits may need adjustment to better serve our current needs and aspirations.

Aligning with Personal Growth

As we grow and evolve as individuals, our habits should evolve as well. Our values, interests, and priorities may shift over time. It is crucial to evaluate whether our current habits align with our evolving sense of self and make adjustments as necessary to support our personal growth and development.

Adapting to External Changes

External factors such as career transitions, lifestyle changes, or shifts in relationships can impact our habits. By recognizing these changes and their potential influence on our routines, we can proactively modify our habits to maintain discipline and ensure they remain conducive to our success.

Assessing Habit Effectiveness

Regularly assessing the effectiveness of our habits is key to habit evolution. Reflect on whether your habits are still serving their intended purpose and contributing to your goals. Identify habits that may have become obsolete or ineffective and consider replacing them with more relevant and impactful ones.

Experimentation and Trial

Habit evolution involves a willingness to experiment and try new approaches. Be open to exploring alternative habits or strategies that may better align with your current circumstances and objectives. Embrace a growth mindset and view habit evolution as an opportunity for learning and discovery.

Seeking Feedback and Support

Feedback from trusted individuals or seeking guidance from experts can offer helpful information about habit evolution. Engage in conversations with mentors, coaches, or peers who can offer different perspectives and help identify areas for improvement or adjustment in your habits.

Gradual Changes and Incremental Progress

Habit evolution does not necessarily mean completely overhauling your routines overnight. Instead, focus on making gradual changes and embracing incremental progress. Small adjustments over time can lead to significant improvements and long-term discipline.

Building Resilience in Habit Evolution

Habit evolution requires resilience, as it involves navigating change and potential setbacks. Maintain your dedication to your objectives and recognize that modifying habits may involve a process of experimentation. Embrace resilience by learning from failures, maintaining a positive mindset, and persevering through challenges.

Embracing Lifelong Learning

Habit evolution is an ongoing process throughout life. Embrace a mindset of lifelong learning and growth. Continuously seek new knowledge, explore different perspectives, and adapt your habits accordingly. Remain curious and open to change, as this mindset will support your long-term discipline and success.

By recognizing the importance of habit evolution, regularly assessing your habits, adapting to changing circumstances, and embracing a growth-oriented mindset, you can sustain long-term discipline and continuously align your habits with your evolving goals and aspirations. Habit evolution empowers you to thrive in a dynamic world and unlock your full potential.

Chapter 4

Discipline and Time Management

Maximizing Productivity through Self-Control

Introduction to Time Management

Effective time management is a crucial skill that enables individuals to make the most of their available time, accomplish their goals, and maintain discipline in their lives. It involves planning, organizing, and allocating time to various tasks and activities in a manner that optimizes productivity and minimizes time wastage. Here's a comprehensive explanation of the importance of effective time management and its correlation with discipline.

Achieving Goals

Goal achievement directly correlates with effective time management. By managing time effectively, individuals can allocate dedicated time slots for specific tasks related to their goals. This ensures progress and momentum towards the desired outcomes. Effective time management helps individuals stay focused, prioritize tasks, and take consistent action towards their goals.

Productivity and Efficiency

Time management enhances productivity and efficiency. When individuals have a clear plan and structure for their time, they are more likely to work efficiently and complete tasks within the allocated timeframes. It reduces the likelihood of procrastination, distractions, and time wastage, allowing individuals to make the best use of their available time.

Stress Reduction

Effective time management reduces stress levels. When individuals have a well-organized schedule and allocate time for both work and personal activities, they experience a sense of control and balance. Engaging in such behavior not only alleviates feelings of overwhelm but also promotes a healthier work-life balance.

Discipline and Self-Control

Discipline and time management closely intertwine. Discipline is the ability to adhere to a set of rules, principles, or routines, and time management requires discipline to follow schedules and stick to allocated timeframes. By practicing time management, individuals cultivate self-discipline, which strengthens their ability to maintain focus, resist distractions, and stay committed to their tasks.

Prioritization

Time management involves the skill of prioritization. It requires individuals to identify and prioritize tasks based on their importance and urgency. Through effective time management, individuals learn to distinguish between essential and nonessential tasks, allowing them to focus on what truly matters and align their efforts accordingly.

Increased Accountability

Time management promotes accountability. When individuals manage their time effectively, they become more aware of their responsibilities and deadlines. This heightened sense of accountability helps individuals take ownership of their tasks, meet deadlines, and fulfill commitments.

Improved Decision Making

Time management enhances decision-making skills. When individuals have a clear overview of their time commitments, they can make informed decisions regarding accepting new tasks, delegating responsibilities, or managing their workload. This allows for better decision-making in terms of allocating time and resources effectively.

Personal Development

Time management supports personal development. By managing time effectively, individuals create opportunities to invest in their own growth, whether it's through learning new skills, pursuing hobbies, or engaging in self-care activities. Time management enables individuals to prioritize self-improvement and personal well-being.

Work-Life Balance

Effective time management contributes to a healthy work-life balance. It helps individuals allocate time not only for work-related tasks but also for personal and recreational activities. This balance promotes overall well-being, reduces burnout, and enhances overall satisfaction in both personal and professional domains.

Long-term Success

Time management is a key factor in achieving long-term success. It allows individuals to consistently dedicate time and effort to their goals, ensuring progress and achievement over time. By managing time effectively, individuals lay a foundation for sustained success and personal fulfillment.

Effective time management is essential for achieving goals, enhancing productivity, reducing stress, and maintaining discipline in our lives. It empowers individuals to make the best use of their time, prioritize tasks, and stay focused on what matters most. By recognizing the correlation between discipline and time management, individuals can develop the skills necessary to optimize their time, accomplish their goals, and lead a more balanced and fulfilling life.

The Psychology of Time Management

Time Perception

Time perception is a subjective experience influenced by various psychological factors. Depending on factors such as interest, engagement, and the level of challenge involved, different tasks and activities can make time seem to pass quickly or drag on. Understanding these subjective perceptions of time can help individuals better manage their time and maintain discipline.

Task Complexity and Time Estimation

The complexity of a task can impact time perception. Difficult or unfamiliar tasks may feel more time-consuming, leading individuals to underestimate the time required. Such behaviors can result in poor time management if individuals fail to allocate sufficient time for complex tasks. Developing an awareness of task complexity and adjusting time estimates accordingly is essential for effective time management.

Attention and Time

The quality of attention individuals devote to tasks affects their perception of time. When fully engaged and focused on a task, individuals may enter a state of flow where time seems to pass quickly. On the other hand, when attention is divided or distracted, time can appear to drag. Cultivating focused attention and minimizing distractions are key to managing time effectively.

Procrastination and Time

Procrastination is a common psychological behavior that can significantly impact time management. Procrastinators tend to delay tasks, leading to a sense of time pressure and last-minute rush. Understanding the psychological factors behind procrastination, such as fear of failure or discomfort, can help individuals overcome this behavior and develop discipline in managing their time.

Delayed Gratification and Time Perspective

The ability to delay gratification is crucial for effective time management. Individuals who prioritize long-term rewards over immediate gratification demonstrate greater discipline in managing their time. Developing a future-oriented time perspective and focusing on the long-term benefits of disciplined time management can help individuals resist short-term distractions.

Self-Control and Time Management

Self-control plays a fundamental role in managing time effectively. It involves resisting temptations, staying focused on tasks, and adhering to planned schedules. Building self-control requires discipline and the ability to regulate impulses. Developing strategies to enhance self-control, such as setting specific goals, breaking tasks into manageable segments, and practicing mindfulness, can strengthen time management skills.

Overcoming Procrastination

Procrastination is often a result of a lack of self-control and discipline. Overcoming procrastination requires understanding its underlying causes and implementing strategies to counteract it. Techniques such as breaking tasks into smaller, more manageable parts, setting deadlines, and using accountability systems can help individuals overcome procrastination and improve their time management.

Emotional Regulation and Time Management

Emotional regulation skills are essential for effective time management. Emotions such as stress, anxiety, or boredom can disrupt focus and hinder productivity. Developing strategies to manage emotions, such as mindfulness, stress reduction techniques, and creating a positive work environment, can support disciplined time management.

Self-Awareness and Time Management

Self-awareness is a critical component of effective time management. Understanding personal strengths, weaknesses, and patterns of behavior helps individuals identify areas for improvement and tailor their time management strategies accordingly. Regular self-reflection, self-assessment, and seeking feedback from others can enhance self-awareness and inform effective time management practices.

Motivation and Time Management

Motivation serves as a driving force behind disciplined time management. Individuals who discover motivation and meaning in their tasks are more likely to manage their time effectively. Cultivating intrinsic motivation, setting meaningful goals, and finding ways to stay inspired can fuel discipline and enhance time-management skills.

The psychology of time management encompasses various factors that influence our perception of time and our ability to manage it effectively. Understanding the psychological aspects of time perception, the impact of self-control and discipline, and strategies for overcoming procrastination and managing emotions are essential for maximizing productivity and achieving goals. By harnessing these psychological insights, individuals can develop the discipline needed to make the most of their time and lead more fulfilling lives.

Setting Clear Goals and Priorities

The Power of Clear Goals

Clear goals provide direction and purpose in managing time effectively. They serve as a roadmap, guiding individuals towards their desired outcomes. By setting clear and specific goals, individuals can align their time and efforts with what truly matters to them, increasing motivation and discipline.

SMART Goal Framework

The SMART goal framework is widely used for setting clear and effective goals. SMART stands for Specific, Measurable, Achievable, Relevant, and Time-bound. Setting goals that meet these criteria provides clarity and enables individuals to track progress and make adjustments as needed.

Long-Term and Short-Term Goals

Effective time management involves setting both long-term and short-term goals. Long-term goals provide a big-picture vision, while short-term goals break down the larger objectives into actionable steps. By setting milestones and smaller goals along the way, individuals can stay focused, maintain discipline, and make steady progress towards their ultimate objectives.

Prioritization Techniques

Prioritization is essential in managing time effectively. It involves identifying tasks and activities that have the highest value and allocating time accordingly. One popular technique is the Eisenhower Matrix, which categorizes tasks into four quadrants based on urgency and importance. This helps individuals prioritize tasks and focus on what is truly meaningful and impactful.

Value-Based Prioritization

Prioritizing tasks based on personal values ensures that time is spent on activities that align with one's core beliefs and priorities. By clarifying personal values and aligning tasks accordingly, individuals can make more intentional choices about how they allocate their time and maintain discipline in pursuing what truly matters to them.

Time Blocking

Timeblocking is a technique where individuals allocate specific time blocks for different tasks or activities. By scheduling dedicated time slots for specific priorities, individuals create structure and ensure that important tasks receive focused attention. Time blocking helps in managing time effectively and avoiding distractions or time wastage.

Pareto Principle

The Pareto Principle, also known as the 80/20 rule, states that roughly 80% of results come from 20% of efforts. Applying this principle to time management involves identifying the key tasks or activities that will yield the most significant results and focusing on them first. By prioritizing high-impact activities, individuals can maximize productivity and achieve desired outcomes.

Review and Adjust

Regularly reviewing goals and priorities is essential to maintain alignment and adapt to changing circumstances. By periodically assessing progress and adjusting priorities as needed, individuals can ensure that their time is spent on tasks that contribute most effectively to their goals. This flexibility allows for continued discipline and responsiveness in time management.

Avoiding Overcommitment

Overcommitment can lead to a lack of focus and effectiveness in time management. It is important to be realistic about the available time and resources and avoid taking on too many tasks or responsibilities. Learning to say no when necessary and setting boundaries can help individuals maintain discipline and allocate their time more effectively.

Time Audit

Conducting a time audit involves tracking and analyzing how time is currently being spent. By examining patterns and identifying time-wasting activities or inefficient practices, individuals can make informed decisions about how to better allocate their time and increase discipline. A time audit helps determine where improvements are needed and facilitates effective time management practices.

Setting clear goals and priorities is crucial for effective time management and maintaining discipline. By adopting techniques such as SMART goals, prioritization methods, and time blocking, individuals can allocate their time wisely and focus on high-value tasks. Regular review, avoidance of overcommitment, and conducting a time audit support ongoing discipline and continuous improvement in time management efforts. With these strategies in place, individuals can maximize productivity, achieve their goals, and lead more fulfilling lives.

Creating Effective Schedules and Routines

Disciplined scheduling plays a crucial role in enhancing productivity and reducing time wastage. There are methods for establishing organized routines that aid in maintaining discipline and managing time effectively.

The Importance of Schedules and Routines

Schedules and routines provide structure and organization to daily activities, enabling individuals to make the most of their time. They create a framework that supports discipline by establishing consistent patterns and allocating time for specific tasks and activities.

Time Blocking

Timeblocking involves dividing the day into dedicated blocks of time for different activities. By assigning specific time slots for tasks, individuals can create a clear schedule that allows for focused work and minimizes distractions. Timeblocking helps maintain discipline by providing a visual representation of how time is allocated throughout the day.

Prioritizing High-Value Activities

When creating schedules and routines, it is important to prioritize high-value activities that align with goals and priorities. By identifying and allocating time for tasks that have the most significant impact, individuals ensure that their efforts are focused on what truly matters, enhancing discipline and productivity.

Establishing Regular Routines

Routines create a sense of consistency and familiarity, making it easier to maintain discipline. By incorporating habits and activities into a daily or weekly routine, individuals streamline their decision-making process and reduce the mental effort required to stay on track.

Flexibility within Structure

While routines provide structure, it is essential to allow for flexibility and adaptability. Unexpected events or changing priorities may require adjustments to the schedule. By building in buffers and allowing for some degree of flexibility, individuals can maintain discipline while being responsive to unforeseen circumstances.

Optimizing Productive Time

Effective scheduling involves identifying peak productivity periods and aligning important or challenging tasks with those. By understanding their personal energy levels and cognitive rhythms, individuals can schedule demanding tasks during their most productive hours, thereby maximizing efficiency and discipline.

Eliminating Time Wasters

Schedules and routines help individuals identify and eliminate time-wasting activities. Individuals can free up valuable time for more meaningful tasks by consciously evaluating how they spend their time and eliminating or minimizing activities that do not contribute to their goals or priorities. This process requires discipline in recognizing and curbing unproductive behaviors.

Incorporating Breaks and Rest

Schedules should include intentional breaks and designated time for rest. Taking regular breaks helps maintain focus, prevent burnout, and enhance overall productivity and discipline. By scheduling breaks and adhering to them, individuals ensure they receive the necessary mental and physical rejuvenation to maintain discipline throughout the day.

Planning for Personal Well-being

Effective scheduling involves allocating time specifically for self-care and personal well-being. Engaging in activities that promote physical and mental well-being, such as exercise, relaxation, and hobbies, supports overall discipline and productivity. By consciously scheduling time for self-care, individuals prioritize their health and improve their ability to maintain discipline.

Regular Evaluation and Adjustment

Schedules and routines should be regularly evaluated to ensure their effectiveness. Periodically reviewing the schedule, identifying areas for improvement, and making necessary adjustments based on changing circumstances or priorities supports the ongoing discipline and optimization of time management efforts.

Creating effective schedules and routines plays a vital role in maximizing productivity and maintaining discipline. By incorporating techniques such as time blocking, prioritization, flexibility, and regular evaluation, individuals can establish structured routines that support discipline and effective time management. Individuals can enhance their productivity and achieve their goals more efficiently by adhering to schedules and making intentional choices about time allocation.

Overcoming Procrastination

The Nature of Procrastination

Procrastination is the tendency to delay or avoid tasks and activities that require effort or are perceived as unpleasant. It often stems from factors such as fear of failure, perfectionism, lack of motivation, or feeling overwhelmed. Procrastination can significantly impact time management by causing delays, decreased productivity, and increased stress.

Recognizing Procrastination Patterns

The first step in overcoming procrastination is to become aware of one's procrastination patterns. This involves identifying the tasks or situations that trigger procrastination and understanding the underlying reasons for the avoidance behavior. By recognizing the patterns, individuals can take proactive steps to address them.

Setting Clear and Specific Goals

Clear and specific goals provide a sense of direction and purpose, making it easier to stay focused and motivated. By breaking larger tasks into smaller, manageable steps and setting deadlines for each, individuals create a roadmap that minimizes the tendency to procrastinate.

Utilizing Time Management Techniques

Time management techniques such as prioritization, time blocking, and creating to-do lists can help overcome procrastination. By organizing tasks, assigning specific time slots, and breaking them down into smaller, achievable portions, individuals can enhance discipline and maintain focus on the most important tasks.

Developing Effective Strategies for Task Initiation

Task initiation is often a significant hurdle for procrastinators. To overcome this, individuals can employ strategies such as the "two-minute rule"—starting a task and committing to working on it for just two minutes. Starting a task can often be the most challenging part, but once you build the initial momentum, it becomes easier to continue.

Implementing the Pomodoro Technique

The Pomodoro Technique divides work into 25-minute segments, interspersed with brief breaks. This structured approach helps overcome procrastination by providing a clear timeframe for focused work, while the breaks prevent burnout and maintain motivation. By adhering to this technique, individuals build discipline and productivity.

Practicing Self-Reflection and Goal Alignment

Regular self-reflection allows individuals to evaluate their motivations, values, and long-term goals. By aligning tasks with personal values and understanding the importance of completing them, individuals can foster intrinsic motivation and discipline, making it easier to overcome procrastination.

Utilizing Accountability Systems

Accountability can be a powerful tool in overcoming procrastination. Sharing goals and progress with others, whether through an accountability partner, coach, or online community, creates a sense of responsibility and encourages individuals to stay on track. Knowing that someone else is aware of their commitments helps build discipline and minimizes the tendency to procrastinate.

Breaking Tasks into Smaller Steps

Procrastination often stems from feeling overwhelmed by the magnitude of a task. Dividing tasks into smaller, more manageable steps alleviates the perceived burden and facilitates initiation. By focusing on one step at a time, individuals can build momentum and gradually work through the task.

Cultivating a Positive Mindset

Overcoming procrastination requires cultivating a positive mindset and reframing negative thoughts. By focusing on the benefits and rewards of completing tasks, individuals can increase their motivation and discipline. Embracing a growth mindset, which recognizes that effort and progress are more important than perfection, reduces the fear of failure and supports discipline in tackling tasks.

Overcoming procrastination is essential for effective time management and maintaining discipline. By understanding the psychological reasons behind procrastination and implementing strategies such as setting clear goals, utilizing time management techniques, developing effective task initiation strategies, practicing self-reflection, and leveraging accountability systems, individuals can overcome procrastination and build self-discipline. By consistently applying these strategies, individuals can stay focused on tasks, enhance productivity, and achieve their goals more efficiently.

Time Blocking and Task Chunking

Understanding Time Blocking

Time blocking is a time management technique that involves allocating dedicated blocks of time to specific tasks or activities. It helps individuals prioritize their activities, create a structured schedule, and minimize distractions. By designating specific time slots for different tasks, individuals can enhance focus, productivity, and discipline.

Benefits of Time Blocking

Time blocking offers several benefits for discipline and productivity. It provides a clear visual representation of how time is allocated throughout the day, ensuring that important tasks receive adequate attention. It also helps individuals avoid multitasking and distractions by dedicating focused time to each task. Time blocking promotes discipline by creating a sense of commitment and accountability for adhering to the scheduled activities.

Breaking Down Tasks

Task chunking is the practice of breaking down larger tasks into smaller, more manageable segments. It allows individuals to tackle complex projects or assignments without feeling overwhelmed. By breaking tasks into smaller chunks, individuals can maintain focus and concentration, as well as build a sense of progress and accomplishment with each completed segment.

Enhanced Focus and Productivity

Task chunking enhances focus by providing clear objectives for each segment. It prevents individuals from feeling overwhelmed by the entirety of a large task and allows them to concentrate on one segment at a time. With focused attention, individuals can devote their energy and resources more effectively, leading to increased productivity and efficient task completion.

Time Efficiency

Chunking tasks into smaller segments enables individuals to make better use of their time. By breaking tasks down, it becomes easier to identify dependencies, allocate appropriate time for each segment, and allocate resources efficiently. This approach helps individuals optimize their schedules and make the most of their available time.

Overcoming Procrastination

Task chunking can help overcome procrastination by making assignments more approachable. When faced with a daunting or overwhelming task, individuals may be more prone to procrastination. However, by breaking it down into manageable chunks, it becomes easier to initiate and progress through the task, reducing the likelihood of procrastination.

Increased Task Completion Rate

Chunking tasks improves focus and increases the likelihood of completing them. The completion of smaller, more manageable segments encourages a sense of development and accomplishment. This sense of achievement boosts motivation and discipline, driving individuals to continue working through the remaining chunks.

Flexibility and Adaptability

Time blocking and task chunking provide a framework that allows for flexibility and adaptability. While time blocks provide a general structure, they can be adjusted as needed to accommodate unexpected events or changes in priorities. Task chunking allows individuals to rearrange or reprioritize smaller segments within a task without disrupting the overall schedule, making it easier to adapt to changing circumstances.

Minimizing Decision Fatigue

Time blocking and task chunking reduce decision fatigue by providing a clear plan and structure. Instead of constantly deciding what to work on next, individuals can refer to their pre-planned schedule and focus on executing the tasks within each time block. This method reduces decision-making stress and frees up mental energy for more important tasks.

Improved Work-Life Balance

Time blocking and task chunking contribute to improved work-life balance by helping individuals allocate dedicated time for both professional and personal activities. By intentionally setting aside time for relaxation, hobbies, and self-care, individuals can maintain discipline in managing their time and ensure they prioritize activities that contribute to their overall well-being.

Time blocking and task chunking are powerful techniques for enhancing discipline, focus, and productivity. By allocating specific time blocks to tasks and breaking them down into manageable segments, individuals can maximize their efficiency, overcome procrastination, and maintain discipline in managing their time. These strategies provide a structured approach to time management, improve work-life balance, and enable individuals to accomplish their goals effectively.

Managing Distractions

Identifying Common Distractions

Distractions can significantly impact discipline and time management. Common distractions include social media notifications, email alerts, excessive noise, interruptions from colleagues or family members, and personal obligations. It is essential to identify these distractions to effectively manage and minimize their impact on productivity.

Creating a Distraction-Free Environment

One effective technique for managing distractions is to create a distraction-free environment. This involves setting up a dedicated workspace that is free from potential distractions. Minimizing visual and auditory distractions, such as turning off notifications on electronic devices or using noise-canceling headphones, can help maintain focus and discipline.

Timeboxing

Timeboxing is a technique that involves allocating specific time blocks for focused work. During these time blocks, individuals commit to working on a single task without any distractions. Setting clear boundaries and dedicating uninterrupted time minimizes distractions and fosters discipline.

Implementing Digital Detox

Digital devices can be major sources of distraction. Setting designated periods of time to turn off or put away electronic devices is a key component of implementing a digital detox strategy. This strategy enables individuals to concentrate exclusively on the current task, preventing them from succumbing to the temptation of continuously checking emails, social media, or other online platforms.

Prioritizing Tasks

Effective task prioritization helps minimize distractions by focusing on the most important and high-value tasks. By identifying and prioritizing tasks based on their importance and urgency, individuals can allocate their time and attention accordingly, reducing the likelihood of getting distracted by less critical activities.

Practicing Mindfulness

Mindfulness is a powerful technique for managing distractions. By cultivating present-moment awareness, individuals can better recognize when distractions arise and consciously redirect their attention back to the task at hand. Mindfulness also enhances self-control and discipline, allowing individuals to resist the urge to engage in distracting activities.

Setting Boundaries

Establishing clear boundaries with colleagues, family members, or roommates is essential for minimizing interruptions and distractions. Communicate your need for focused work time and request cooperation in maintaining a quiet and distraction-free environment during those periods.

Utilizing Productivity Tools

Various productivity tools and apps can help manage distractions. These tools can block distracting websites or apps, provide time-tracking and goal-setting features, and generate reports on productivity levels. Utilizing such tools can assist in maintaining discipline and staying focused on important tasks.

Implementing the Pomodoro Technique

The Pomodoro Technique involves working in focused sprints, typically 25 minutes, followed by short breaks. The focused work intervals minimize distractions and provide complete attention to the task. This technique allows individuals to manage their energy levels, maintain discipline, and work efficiently in shorter, dedicated bursts.

Practicing Self-Discipline

Ultimately, managing distractions requires self-discipline. It is essential to develop self-awareness and recognize when distractions arise. By consciously choosing to redirect attention and resist the pull of distractions, individuals can cultivate self-discipline and strengthen their ability to stay focused and productive.

Managing distractions is critical to sustaining discipline and effective time management. By identifying common distractions, creating a distraction-free environment, utilizing techniques such as timeboxing and digital detox, prioritizing tasks, practicing mindfulness, setting boundaries, leveraging productivity tools, implementing the Pomodoro Technique, and cultivating self-discipline, individuals can minimize distractions and foster a focused work environment that supports discipline and productivity.

Effective Prioritization and Decision-Making

Understanding the Importance of Prioritization: Prioritization is key to effective time management. It involves assessing tasks and activities based on their importance and urgency to determine the order in which they should be addressed. By prioritizing tasks, individuals can allocate their time and resources more efficiently, ensuring that the most critical and valuable ones are completed first.

Assessing Task Importance and Urgency

When prioritizing tasks, it is critical to take into account both their importance and urgency. Important tasks are those that align with long-term goals and have a significant impact on desired outcomes. Urgent tasks require immediate attention and have imminent deadlines. By assessing the importance and urgency of tasks, individuals can make informed decisions about how to allocate their time and prioritize effectively.

Utilizing Time Management Techniques

Various time management techniques can aid in prioritization and decision-making. The Eisenhower Matrix, for example, categorizes tasks into four quadrants based on their importance and urgency: important and urgent, important but not urgent, urgent but not relevant, and not urgent or important. This technique helps individuals identify and prioritize tasks accordingly.

Applying Pareto Principle

The Pareto Principle, also known as the 80/20 rule, states that roughly 80% of the outcomes result from 20% of the inputs. Applied to time management, it suggests that a significant portion of productivity comes from a few key tasks. By identifying and focusing on the most impactful tasks, individuals can maximize their productivity and time usage.

Considering Long-Term Goals

Prioritization should align with long-term goals and objectives. When making decisions about which tasks to prioritize, individuals should consider how each one contributes to their overarching goals. Individuals can ensure meaningful progress by prioritizing tasks that directly support long-term success.

Evaluating Resource Allocation

Effective prioritization requires considering the available resources, such as time, energy, and skills. It involves assessing the feasibility and practicality of completing tasks within the given constraints. By realistically evaluating resource allocation, individuals can make informed decisions about how to best utilize their available resources.

Using Decision-Making Frameworks

Decision-making frameworks provide a structured approach to making choices. For example, the SWOT analysis (Strengths, Weaknesses, Opportunities, and Threats) helps assess the pros and cons of different options. By employing decision-making frameworks, individuals can systematically evaluate options, consider the potential outcomes, and make informed decisions that align with their priorities.

Avoiding Analysis Paralysis

Overthinking and indecision can hinder effective prioritization. It is important to strike a balance between gathering necessary information and taking decisive action. To prevent analysis paralysis, establish reasonable time limits for decision-making and concentrate on the key factors that influence prioritization.

Seeking Input and Feedback

In complex decision-making situations, seeking input and feedback from trusted individuals can provide valuable insights. Consultation with colleagues, mentors, or subject matter experts can help clarify priorities and enhance decision-making. Gathering diverse perspectives can uncover blind spots and lead to more well-rounded decisions.

Regularly Reassessing Priorities

Priorities may change over time due to shifting circumstances, new information, or evolving goals. It is important to regularly reassess and adjust priorities accordingly. Individuals can invest their time and energy in the most relevant and impactful tasks by periodically reviewing and updating their priorities.

Effective prioritization and decision-making are essential components of disciplined time management. By assessing task importance and urgency, utilizing time management techniques, aligning decisions with long-term goals, considering available resources, employing decision-making frameworks, avoiding analysis paralysis, seeking input and feedback, and regularly reassessing priorities, individuals can optimize their time usage and make informed choices that support discipline and productivity.

Enhancing Time Efficiency

Minimizing Multitasking

Multitasking can lead to decreased productivity and increased errors. By focusing on one task at a time, individuals can maintain better concentration and produce higher-quality work. Prioritizing tasks and dedicating specific time blocks for each task allows for greater efficiency and concentration.

Delegating Tasks

Effective delegation is a valuable time management skill. Delegating tasks to competent individuals frees up time for higher-priority responsibilities. It entails pinpointing tasks suitable for delegation to others while maintaining transparent communication and accountability to guarantee successful completion.

Utilizing Productivity Tools

Numerous productivity tools are available to help individuals manage their time effectively. These tools range from digital calendars and task management apps to time-tracking software and project management platforms. Utilizing such tools can aid in organizing tasks, setting reminders, and monitoring progress, ultimately enhancing time efficiency.

Time Blocking

Time blocking involves dedicating specific times to particular tasks or activities. By scheduling uninterrupted blocks of time for focused work, individuals can eliminate distractions and increase productivity. Timeblocking can be combined with the Pomodoro Technique, which involves working in short bursts with scheduled breaks to maintain focus and prevent burnout.

Setting Boundaries and Saying No

Establishing boundaries and learning to say no to nonessential tasks or commitments is crucial for time efficiency. It involves prioritizing one's own goals and needs and being selective about the tasks and activities taken on. By setting clear boundaries and managing commitments, individuals can protect their time and allocate it to activities that align with their priorities.

Streamlining Processes

Streamlining processes involves identifying and eliminating inefficiencies in workflows. By analyzing tasks and identifying areas for improvement, individuals can streamline processes, eliminate redundant steps, and optimize time usage. Such efforts could include automating repetitive tasks, creating templates, or implementing standardized procedures.

Avoiding Procrastination

Procrastination can significantly hinder time efficiency. Recognizing the causes of procrastination, such as fear of failure or overwhelm, is essential for overcoming it. Strategies like breaking tasks into smaller, manageable steps, setting deadlines, and using accountability systems help combat procrastination and improve time management.

Eliminating Time-Wasting Habits

Time-wasting habits, such as excessive social media use or unnecessary web browsing, can consume valuable time. Developing self-discipline and awareness of these habits is key to eliminating them. Implementing techniques like setting designated times for checking emails or using website blockers can help minimize distractions and reclaim lost time.

Time Audit

Conducting a time audit entails monitoring current time usage to pinpoint areas of inefficiency or time leakage. By analyzing daily activities and their time consumption, individuals can identify patterns, prioritize tasks, and make adjustments to enhance time efficiency. A time audit reveals advantageous information about time management habits and highlights areas for improvement.

Continuous Learning and Improvement

Continuous learning and improvement can refine time efficiency as a skill. Staying updated on time management techniques, seeking productivity resources, and adopting new strategies can help individuals refine their approach to time management. Regular self-reflection and adjustment of strategies based on personal experiences can lead to continuous improvement in time efficiency.

Enhancing time efficiency requires a combination of effective techniques and self-discipline. By minimizing multitasking, delegating tasks, utilizing productivity tools, time blocking, setting boundaries, streamlining processes, avoiding procrastination, eliminating time-wasting habits, conducting a time audit, and embracing continuous learning, individuals can maximize their productivity and achieve greater success in managing their time effectively.

Continuous Improvement and Adaptation

Reflecting on Time Management Practices

Regular reflection on time management practices is essential for continuous improvement. Taking time to evaluate how well certain strategies are working and identifying areas for improvement allows individuals to refine their approach. It entails analyzing successful strategies, identifying areas for improvement, and formulating adjustments to boost productivity and discipline.

Seeking Feedback and Learning from Others

Seeking feedback from colleagues, mentors, or trusted individuals can provide valuable insights and alternative perspectives. Others may offer suggestions or techniques that have worked for them, helping individuals refine their time management strategies. Learning from the experiences and successes of others allows for continuous improvement and adaptation.

Embracing Flexibility

Flexibility is a key element in effective time management. Recognizing that plans may change and that unexpected circumstances may arise helps individuals adapt to new situations without compromising discipline. Being open to adjusting schedules, priorities, and approaches when necessary allows for better time management and the ability to stay on track despite unforeseen events.

Embracing Technology

Technology can be a valuable tool for continuous improvement in time management. Staying updated on new productivity apps, software, or tools can offer innovative ways to enhance efficiency. Experimenting with different digital tools, automation features, or time-tracking apps can help individuals identify and adopt technologies that align with their needs and support discipline.

Regular Review of Goals

Regularly reviewing and reassessing goals is important for staying focused and maintaining discipline. As circumstances change, priorities may shift, and goals may need to be adjusted. By periodically evaluating goals and ensuring they are still relevant and aligned with overall objectives, individuals can make necessary adjustments to optimize their time management efforts.

Experimenting with Time Management Techniques

There is no universal approach to time management. Individuals should be open to experimenting with different techniques and strategies to discover what works best for them. Trying out different productivity methods, scheduling approaches, or prioritization techniques allows for continuous improvement by identifying the most effective practices for personal productivity and discipline.

Learning from Mistakes and Setbacks

Mistakes and setbacks are valuable learning opportunities. When time management efforts fall short, it is important to analyze what went wrong and identify areas for improvement. By learning from mistakes and setbacks, individuals can make adjustments and develop resilience to maintain discipline in the face of challenges.

Cultivating a Growth Mindset

Adopting a growth mindset is crucial for continuous improvement in time management. Individuals can approach time management as a learning journey by embracing the belief that skills and abilities can develop through effort and practice. Viewing challenges as opportunities for growth and seeing setbacks as temporary rather than permanent failures supports ongoing improvement and adaptation.

Regular Evaluation of Time Allocation

Regularly evaluating how time is allocated is essential for determining which areas need enhancement. People should examine the amount of time they dedicate to various activities and determine if it matches their priorities. Adjustments can be made to allocate more time to high-value tasks and eliminate or delegate low-priority activities to optimize time usage.

Emphasizing Work-Life Balance

Maintaining a healthy work-life balance is crucial for sustained discipline and optimal time management. Recognizing the importance of rest, leisure, and self-care allows individuals to recharge and maintain productivity. Balancing work responsibilities with personal well-being ensures that time is used efficiently and effectively, promoting long-term discipline.

Continuous improvement and adaptation are vital for optimizing time usage and maintaining discipline. By reflecting on time management practices, seeking feedback, embracing flexibility, leveraging technology, regularly reviewing goals, experimenting with techniques, learning from mistakes, cultivating a growth mindset, evaluating time allocation, and emphasizing work-life balance, individuals can continually refine their approach to time management and enhance their overall productivity and discipline.

Chapter 5

Mastering Delayed Gratification

The Role of Discipline in Long-Term Success

Understanding Delayed Gratification

Delayed gratification is the ability to resist the temptation of an immediate reward in favor of a greater, more meaningful reward that will come later. It requires self-control, patience, and discipline, all of which are vital skills for achieving long-term success. In our fast-paced world, where instant gratification is often readily available, the ability to delay gratification has become a rare yet valuable trait. Those who master it can often set themselves apart in both personal and professional spheres.

At the heart of delayed gratification is the understanding that most significant goals—whether they involve financial success, health, or personal growth—are not achieved overnight. They require sustained effort, long-term planning, and the ability to forgo short-term pleasures to stay focused on long-term objectives. For instance, someone saving for retirement must consistently resist the temptation to spend their money on frivolous purchases in the present, choosing instead to invest in their future.

Delayed gratification doesn't come naturally to most people. Our brains are wired to seek immediate rewards because they provide a quick hit of dopamine, the "feel-good" hormone. This tendency toward instant gratification can make it difficult to stay disciplined in pursuing long-term goals. However, with practice, individuals can strengthen their ability to delay gratification and make choices that better align with their long-term aspirations.

When you master delayed gratification, you develop the discipline to resist distractions and stay committed to your goals, even when the rewards aren't immediately visible. This process of self-control improves your focus and productivity and enhances your ability to persevere in the face of challenges. People who master this skill are more likely to maintain their motivation over the long term, which is essential for achieving success in any area of life.

The Marshmallow Test and Its Implications

One of the most famous studies on delayed gratification is the Marshmallow Test, conducted by psychologist Walter Mischel in the late 1960s. In this experiment, young children were given a choice: they could either eat one marshmallow immediately or wait for 15 minutes and receive two marshmallows as a reward. The study measured the children's ability to delay gratification and resist the immediate reward in favor of a larger, delayed reward.

Years later, follow-up studies revealed that the children who were able to wait for the second marshmallow tended to experience more success in various aspects of life, including higher academic achievement, better health, and stronger interpersonal relationships. These findings suggest that the ability to delay gratification is a powerful predictor of long-term success and personal fulfillment.

The Marshmallow Test highlights the importance of self-discipline in overcoming the impulse for immediate rewards. Those who succeeded in the test weren't necessarily smarter or more talented than their peers—they simply had better self-control and were willing to wait for a greater reward. This finding underscores the idea that discipline is a skill that can be learned and applied to any area of life.

The implications of this study extend far beyond childhood. Even in adulthood, the ability to delay gratification plays a key role in success. Whether it's saving for retirement, working toward a promotion, or training for a marathon, the ability to forgo short-term pleasures in favor of long-term gains is essential. The Marshmallow Test serves as a powerful reminder that those who are disciplined enough to wait often experience greater rewards in the long run.

The lesson here is clear: the rewards of patience and discipline can be profound. While the temptation to indulge in immediate gratification is strong, the benefits of delaying that gratification—better health, greater success, and a deeper sense of accomplishment—far outweigh the fleeting pleasures of the moment.

The Power of Patience

Patience is a core component of delayed gratification, and mastering it can dramatically improve your ability to achieve long-term goals. Patience allows individuals to maintain focus and perseverance, even when progress is slow or rewards seem distant. In a world where we are conditioned to expect quick results, cultivating patience requires a significant shift in mindset, but it is a skill that can be developed over time.

Patience also plays a critical role in decision-making. Those who lack patience tend to make impulsive decisions based on short-term desires, often leading to less favorable outcomes. In contrast, disciplined individuals with a long-term perspective can wait for the right opportunity, make thoughtful decisions, and achieve better results in the long run.

For example, consider the process of investing in the stock market. Investors who panic and sell at the first sign of a market downturn often miss out on the long-term gains that patient investors enjoy. Over time, those who maintain discipline and endure volatility typically reap higher returns. This concept applies to many areas of life, where patience allows you to endure short-term discomfort or setbacks in favor of achieving lasting success.

The psychological benefits of cultivating patience go beyond better decision-making. Patience helps individuals manage stress and frustration, two emotions that often derail disciplined behavior. When you're able to remain patient, you can approach challenges with a calm and focused mindset, which improves your ability to stay disciplined in the face of adversity.

In short, patience provides the mental and emotional foundation for delayed gratification. Patience can help you stay on track, even when the journey is hard or the rewards are far off.

Overcoming Instant Gratification Bias

Instant gratification bias is the tendency to prioritize immediate rewards over long-term benefits. This bias is deep-rooted in human psychology, as our brains are wired to seek pleasure and avoid pain in the short term. However, overcoming this bias is essential for building discipline and achieving meaningful, long-term success.

One way to overcome instant gratification bias is through mindfulness. Mindfulness involves being fully present in the moment and aware of your thoughts, emotions, and impulses. By practicing mindfulness, you can become more aware of when you are tempted to pursue immediate gratification and make a conscious decision to resist. For example, if you find yourself reaching for a sugary snack when you're trying to maintain a healthy diet, mindfulness allows you to pause, reflect on your goals, and choose to delay the gratification in favor of your long-term health.

Goal visualization is another powerful technique for overcoming instant gratification bias. By vividly imagining the long-term rewards of staying disciplined, you can reinforce your commitment to your goals. For instance, if you're saving money for a vacation, visualizing yourself enjoying it in the future can help you resist the temptation to spend on unnecessary purchases in the present. The clearer and more emotionally engaging the visualization, the easier it becomes to resist immediate temptations.

Another strategy is pre-commitment, which involves creating barriers to instant gratification. For example, if you know that you're likely to procrastinate on a task, you can pre-commit by telling a friend or colleague about your deadline, thereby creating external accountability. Pre-commitment helps reduce the likelihood of succumbing to temptations by making it more difficult to indulge in them.

Building awareness of your triggers for instant gratification and actively resisting them through mindfulness, goal visualization, and pre-commitment can help you develop the discipline needed to stay focused on your long-term goals. As you practice these strategies, resisting short-term temptations becomes easier, and you begin to see the value of delaying gratification.

Building Willpower and Self-Control

Willpower and self-control are central to mastering delayed gratification. Willpower is the mental energy required to resist temptations and impulses, while self-control is the ability to regulate your behavior in alignment with your goals. Developing these skills is essential for maintaining discipline and staying focused on long-term objectives.

One effective way to build willpower is through mindfulness training. Mindfulness strengthens your ability to stay present and resist distractions, which helps conserve willpower. By practicing mindfulness regularly, you can become more aware of your impulses and learn to manage them effectively.

Self-regulation strategies are another crucial aspect of building self-control. These strategies involve setting clear boundaries and rules for yourself to prevent impulsive behavior. For example, if you're trying to limit your screen time, setting a rule to only check your phone during designated times of the day can help reduce the temptation to constantly scroll through social media.

Like a muscle, willpower can be strengthened through small, incremental challenges. Starting with minor tasks, such as delaying a small pleasure (like waiting five minutes before eating a snack), builds your willpower gradually. Over time, this practice of delaying small gratifications helps prepare you for larger, more challenging situations where stronger self-control is needed.

Building self-control also requires habit formation. By creating structured routines around key behaviors, you can reduce the need for willpower in daily decisions. For example, if your goal is to exercise regularly, establishing a morning routine that includes a workout reduces the mental energy required to make the decision every day—it becomes a habit rather than a choice.

Strengthening willpower and self-control through these practices allows you to better manage distractions and temptations, making it easier to delay gratification and stay disciplined in pursuit of long-term success.

Developing a Long-Term Perspective

Developing a long-term perspective is crucial for resisting instant gratification and maintaining discipline. It involves shifting focus from immediate rewards to the bigger picture and considering the long-term consequences of our actions. Cultivating a future-oriented mindset allows individuals to make choices that align with their long-term goals and values. Here are strategies to develop a long-term perspective and strengthen discipline:

Setting meaningful and compelling goals is essential for cultivating a long-term perspective. When individuals have clear, meaningful goals that they are passionate about, they are more likely to prioritize long-term benefits over short-term gratification. By reflecting on their values and aspirations, individuals can set goals that inspire them to stay disciplined and committed to their journey.

Visualizing long-term outcomes is a powerful technique to strengthen a long-term perspective. By vividly imagining the future they desire, individuals can create a compelling mental image that serves as a reminder of the rewards awaiting them. Visualization helps individuals connect emotionally with their goals and reinforces their determination to resist instant gratification in pursuit of greater long-term success.

Practicing patience and delayed gratification exercises is instrumental in developing a long-term perspective. Engaging in activities that require waiting, such as delaying a pleasurable activity or saving money for a future purchase, trains individuals to tolerate temporary discomfort for long-term benefits. These exercises build resilience and strengthen the ability to resist immediate rewards in favor of more significant, delayed ones.

Cultivating mindfulness and present-moment awareness supports the development of a long-term perspective. By being fully present in the current moment, individuals can make conscious choices that align with their long-term goals. Mindfulness helps individuals recognize the fleeting nature of instant gratification and encourages them to consider the broader impact of their actions on their future selves.

Engaging in regular reflection and self-assessment fosters a long-term perspective. By regularly evaluating their progress toward their goals, individuals can identify areas for improvement and make necessary adjustments. Reflecting on past experiences and learning from mistakes helps individuals stay focused on long-term growth and reinforces the importance of disciplined decision-making.

Surrounding oneself with individuals who embody a long-term perspective can provide support and inspiration. Being part of a community or seeking mentorship from individuals who have successfully achieved long-term goals can motivate and reinforce the value of delayed gratification. Interacting with like-minded individuals who prioritize long-term success can strengthen discipline and provide a sense of accountability.

Developing a habit of practicing gratitude helps cultivate a long-term perspective. By focusing on the present moment and acknowledging the blessings and progress already achieved, individuals gain perspective on the bigger picture. Gratitude fosters contentment and reduces the inclination to seek immediate gratification, as individuals recognize and appreciate the abundance they already have.

Engaging in long-term planning and strategizing is vital to creating a long-term perspective. By breaking down long-term goals into actionable steps and creating a roadmap, individuals can maintain focus on the ultimate objective. Setting milestones and regularly reviewing progress allows individuals to see the bigger picture and stay disciplined in the face of short-term temptations.

Educating oneself about the benefits of delayed gratification and the pitfalls of instant gratification strengthens the commitment to a long-term perspective. Understanding the psychological and societal consequences of prioritizing immediate rewards can serve as a reminder of the importance of disciplined decision-making. Reading books, articles, or studies on the topic can provide insights and inspiration to stay on track.

Practicing self-compassion is essential when pursuing a long-term perspective. Recognizing that setbacks and challenges are a natural part of the journey allows individuals to bounce back from failures and continue pursuing their long-term goals. Self-compassion fosters resilience and reduces the likelihood of succumbing to instant gratification as a means of escape or self-soothing.

By adopting a long-term perspective, individuals can resist instant gratification and make choices that align with their long-term goals and values. Cultivating a future-oriented mindset requires strategies such as setting meaningful goals, visualizing long-term outcomes, practicing patience and delayed gratification, cultivating mindfulness, reflecting on progress, surrounding oneself with like-minded individuals, practicing gratitude, engaging in long-term planning, educating oneself, and practicing self-compassion. Embracing a long-term perspective empowers individuals to maintain discipline and experience the profound rewards of sustained effort and delayed gratification.

Creating Reward Systems

Reward systems can be effective motivational tools for reinforcing delayed gratification and maintaining discipline. By offering incentives that align with long-term goals, individuals can stay motivated and committed to their journey. Here are some techniques for designing effective reward systems.

Identify Meaningful Rewards

When designing a reward system, it is important to choose rewards that hold value and significance for the individual. These rewards can be tangible or intangible, such as treating oneself to a favorite activity, buying a desired item, or taking a well-deserved break. By selecting personally meaningful rewards, individuals are more likely to stay motivated and disciplined.

Link Rewards to Milestones

Instead of relying solely on immediate rewards, it is beneficial to associate rewards with milestones or significant progress towards long-term goals. Breaking down the journey into smaller milestones allows individuals to celebrate achievements along the way, providing a sense of accomplishment and reinforcing the discipline required for long-term success.

Use both Short-Term and Long-Term Rewards

While long-term rewards are important for upholding discipline, incorporating short-term rewards can provide immediate gratification and boost motivation. By including small rewards for meeting daily or weekly targets, individuals experience a sense of progress and are more likely to stay focused and disciplined.

Make Rewards Contingent on Disciplined Behavior

To reinforce the connection between disciplined behavior and rewards, it is important to ensure that rewards are contingent upon meeting specific criteria or demonstrating disciplined actions. This reinforces the idea that delayed gratification and disciplined behavior lead to the attainment of desired rewards.

Make the Rewards Visible

Visual cues can enhance the effectiveness of reward systems. Displaying a visual representation of the rewards, such as a progress chart or a vision board, serves as a constant reminder of what individuals are working towards. This visual reinforcement helps individuals stay motivated, maintain discipline, and resist instant gratification.

Incorporate Intrinsic Rewards

In addition to external rewards, intrinsic rewards play a vital role in maintaining discipline. Intrinsic rewards are the internal satisfaction and fulfillment derived from the process and progress towards a goal. Focusing on the joy of personal growth, self-improvement, and the satisfaction of overcoming challenges can be powerful motivators that sustain discipline over the long term.

Practice delayed rewards

Just as delayed gratification is a central theme in mastering discipline, incorporating delayed rewards can reinforce the importance of patience and self-control. Individuals learn to appreciate the value of delayed gratification and strengthen their ability to resist immediate temptations by intentionally delaying the receipt of a reward until they achieve a certain milestone or goal.

Ensure Fairness and Consistency

A well-designed reward system should be fair and consistent. It is important to establish clear rules and criteria for earning rewards and ensure that they are applied consistently to all individuals involved. Fairness and consistency create a sense of trust and transparency, reinforcing discipline and motivating individuals to stay committed to their long-term goals.

Adjust the Rewards Over Time

As individuals progress towards their goals and their needs and priorities evolve, it is essential to periodically review and adjust the rewards offered. What might have been motivating in the beginning may lose its impact over time. By adapting the rewards to align with changing circumstances and personal growth, individuals can maintain motivation and discipline.

Celebrate Non-Material Rewards

Not all rewards need to be material in nature. Celebrating non-material rewards, such as personal growth, increased self-confidence, or enhanced skills, can be equally powerful in reinforcing discipline. Acknowledging and appreciating the intangible benefits gained through disciplined actions boosts self-esteem and provides intrinsic motivation for continued progress.

By designing reward systems that incorporate meaningful rewards, milestones, a mix of short-term and long-term incentives, visual cues, intrinsic motivation, and fairness, individuals can create a powerful tool to reinforce delayed gratification and maintain discipline. Reward systems serve as reminders of the long-term benefits of disciplined actions and provide the motivation needed to overcome short-term temptations. When aligned with personal values and goals, reward systems become an integral part of the journey towards long-term success and fulfillment.

Managing Impatience and Frustration

The journey of delayed gratification and maintaining discipline can be challenging, as impatience and frustration may arise when faced with setbacks or the slow progress toward long-term goals. Here are some strategies to manage impatience and frustration and sustain discipline:

Cultivate Self-Awareness:

Recognize and acknowledge feelings of impatience and frustration when they arise. Understand that these emotions are normal and part of the process. By developing self-awareness, individuals can better manage their responses and make conscious choices aligned with long-term goals.

Focus on the Process:

Focus on the process and the little steps you take every day rather than just the final result. Embrace the journey and find fulfillment in the progress made. By appreciating the present moment and the effort invested, individuals can stay motivated and maintain discipline.

Set Realistic Expectations:

Impatience often stems from unrealistic expectations. It is important to set realistic timelines and goals that account for the challenges and obstacles along the way. By setting achievable milestones, individuals can celebrate progress and avoid becoming discouraged by slow progress.

Practice Self-Care:

Taking care of physical and mental well-being is essential in managing impatience and frustration. Engage in activities that promote relaxation, such as exercise, meditation, or hobbies. Prioritize rest and self-care to maintain resilience and a positive mindset.

Seek Support:

Reach out to a support network of friends, family, or mentors who can provide guidance, encouragement, and perspective during challenging times. Sharing experiences and discussing struggles with like-minded individuals can provide motivation and reassurance that one is not alone on the journey.

Break Tasks into Manageable Chunks:

Overwhelming tasks can contribute to impatience and frustration. Break down larger tasks into smaller, more manageable chunks. Focus on completing one task at a time, celebrating each accomplishment along the way. This approach helps maintain a sense of progress and boosts motivation.

Practice Mindfulness:

Mindfulness techniques can help manage impatience and frustration by bringing awareness to the present moment and accepting it without judgment. Engage in mindfulness practices such as deep breathing, meditation, or visualization to cultivate patience, reduce stress, and stay grounded.

Reframe Setbacks as Learning Opportunities:

View setbacks and challenges as valuable learning opportunities rather than failures. Embrace the lessons they provide and use them as stepping stones for growth and improvement. Reframing setbacks in a positive light helps maintain perspective and resilience.

Stay Connected to the Purpose:

Continuously remind yourself of the reasons behind your goals. Reconnect with your values and the long-term vision that drives your actions. By staying connected to your purpose, you can find renewed motivation and endurance to overcome impatience and frustration.

Practice Gratitude:

Cultivate a mindset of gratitude by focusing on the positive aspects of the journey. Express gratitude for the progress made, the lessons learned, and the opportunities ahead. Gratitude shifts the focus from what is lacking to what is present, increasing a feeling of accomplishment and reducing impatience.

Managing impatience and frustration requires a combination of self-awareness, self-care, perspective, and mindset. By implementing these strategies, individuals can navigate the challenges of delayed gratification with resilience, sustain discipline, and stay focused on their long-term success. Remember that patience is a skill that can be developed and honed over time, and setbacks are not indicative of failure but rather opportunities for growth.

Celebrating Milestones and Progress

Recognizing and celebrating milestones and progress is a crucial aspect of maintaining discipline and motivation on the path of delayed gratification. Here is a comprehensive explanation of the importance of celebrating achievements and the psychological benefits it brings:

Reinforcement of Discipline:

Celebrating milestones reinforces the discipline and effort invested in achieving long-term goals. It serves as positive feedback that validates the commitment and hard work put into the journey. By recognizing and celebrating achievements, individuals are motivated to continue their disciplined actions.

Boosts Motivation:

Celebrating milestones boosts motivation by providing a sense of accomplishment and progress. It serves as a reminder of the positive outcomes that discipline and delayed gratification can achieve. Celebrating milestones fuels the intrinsic motivation needed to stay focused and continue striving for long-term success.

Enhances Self-Efficacy:

Celebrating milestones builds self-confidence and enhances self-efficacy—the belief in one's ability to achieve goals. Each milestone serves as evidence of personal competence and reinforces the belief that one can overcome challenges and obstacles. This increased self-efficacy further strengthens discipline and resilience.

Provides Positive Reinforcement:

Celebrating milestones and progress provides positive reinforcement for disciplined behavior. It associates the effort and discipline with feelings of satisfaction, joy, and pride. The positive emotions associated with celebration create an intrinsic reward system that reinforces the disciplined actions taken.

Promotes a Growth Mindset:

Celebrating milestones cultivates a growth mindset, which is the conviction that one can develop abilities and intelligence through effort and dedication. By celebrating progress, individuals embrace the belief that improvement is possible and that discipline can lead to continuous growth and success.

Sustains Momentum:

Celebrating milestones helps sustain momentum on the journey of delayed gratification. It breaks the journey into manageable parts and creates markers of progress. Celebrating milestones provides an opportunity to reflect on the distance covered, reignite motivation, and propel individuals forward with renewed energy.

Cultivates Gratitude and a Positive Mindset:

Celebrating milestones cultivates gratitude for the journey and the achievements accomplished. It shifts the focus from what is yet to be achieved to what has been accomplished. This gratitude fosters a positive mindset and a sense of abundance, which further supports discipline and motivation.

Strengthens Resilience:

Celebrating milestones and progress builds resilience by highlighting the ability to overcome challenges and setbacks. It reminds us that we can still make progress even when faced with difficulties. By acknowledging and celebrating achievements, individuals develop a resilient mindset that can withstand future obstacles.

Provides Perspective and Reflection:

Celebrating milestones allows individuals to pause, reflect, and appreciate the progress made. It provides an opportunity to assess the journey, evaluate strategies, and make adjustments if necessary. This reflection enables individuals to learn from their experiences, further refine their discipline, and set new goals for continued growth.

Encourages Sustainable Habits:

Celebrating milestones reinforces the habits and routines that contribute to discipline and delayed gratification. By acknowledging the progress made, individuals reinforce the positive behaviors and actions that have led to success. This encouragement helps solidify the habits necessary for long-term success.

In summary, celebrating milestones and progress is essential for maintaining discipline and motivation on the path of delayed gratification. It reinforces discipline, boosts motivation, enhances self-efficacy, and provides positive reinforcement. Additionally, it promotes a growth mindset, sustains momentum, cultivates gratitude and a positive mindset, strengthens resilience, provides perspective and reflection, and encourages sustainable habits. By regularly celebrating achievements, individuals can stay focused, inspired, and committed to their long-term goals, ensuring continued success on their journey of delayed gratification.

The Role of Discipline in Long-Term Success

In conclusion, mastering delayed gratification is a powerful tool for achieving long-term success and cultivating discipline. Throughout this chapter, we have explored various aspects of delayed gratification and its connection to discipline. Let's summarize the key points and encourage readers to embrace delayed gratification as a transformative approach to achieving their goals.

Delayed gratification refers to the ability to resist immediate rewards in favor of greater long-term benefits. It requires discipline, self-control, and a future-oriented mindset. By postponing instant gratification, individuals can make more informed decisions, pursue higher-value goals, and experience long-term success.

We discussed the famous marshmallow test and its findings, highlighting the correlation between delayed gratification and favorable outcomes in life. Those who demonstrated higher levels of delayed gratification in childhood were found to have better academic performance, higher self-esteem, and improved social and emotional skills.

Patience emerged as a crucial virtue in the journey of delayed gratification. By cultivating patience, individuals can make better decisions, withstand setbacks, and maintain focus on their long-term goals. Patience provides the necessary endurance to overcome challenges and resist the allure of immediate rewards.

Overcoming instant gratification bias requires mindfulness and goal visualization. Being aware of our tendencies to prioritize short-term pleasures and consciously envisioning the long-term benefits helps shift our focus and reinforce the value of delayed gratification. It allows us to make intentional choices aligned with our long-term goals.

Building willpower and self-control is another vital aspect of mastering delayed gratification. Techniques such as mindfulness practice, developing self-regulation strategies, and creating supportive environments contribute to strengthening our willpower muscle. These skills enhance our ability to resist impulsive desires and stay committed to disciplined actions.

Adopting a long-term perspective is key to sustaining discipline and resisting instant gratification. By setting meaningful goals, visualizing long-term outcomes, and regularly reassessing our progress, we can stay motivated and dedicated to our journey. A long-term perspective enables us to appreciate the value of delayed gratification and recognize the incremental steps taken towards our goals.

Creating reward systems that align with our long-term goals is an effective motivational strategy. By designing meaningful rewards for achieving milestones and progress, we reinforce discipline and create positive associations with our disciplined actions. These rewards serve as additional sources of motivation and encouragement along the journey.

Managing impatience and frustration is crucial in maintaining discipline and focus. Strategies such as developing resilience, practicing self-compassion, and seeking support help us navigate through challenges and setbacks. By acknowledging and addressing impatience and frustration, we can rebound stronger and stay committed to our long-term goals.

Lastly, celebrating milestones and progress is an essential practice in sustaining discipline and motivation. By recognizing and appreciating our achievements, we reinforce our discipline, boost motivation, and cultivate a positive mindset. Celebrations provide us with the energy and inspiration to continue our disciplined actions toward long-term success.

In embracing delayed gratification as a powerful tool for achieving our goals and cultivating discipline, we open ourselves up to a world of possibilities. By resisting the allure of immediate rewards and staying committed to our long-term vision, we can achieve remarkable success and personal growth. Mastering delayed gratification requires effort, resilience, and steadfast loyalty, but the rewards are immeasurable.

Let us embrace delayed gratification as a guiding principle in our lives. Let us cultivate discipline, exercise patience, and make conscious choices that align with our long-term goals. By doing so, we unlock the potential within ourselves to create a life of fulfillment, accomplishment, and lasting success. May our journey of delayed gratification be a testament to our resilience, discipline, and unwavering belief in our ability to achieve greatness.

Chapter 6

Overcoming Obstacles and Staying Committed

Identifying Common Obstacles to Discipline

The path to mastering discipline and achieving long-term goals is often filled with challenges. Knowing the many internal and external obstacles is the first step to overcoming them. Common obstacles include procrastination, lack of motivation, self-doubt, fear of failure, and external distractions.

One of the most prevalent internal obstacles is procrastination. Even with the best intentions, many people struggle to start tasks or projects that seem overwhelming or unpleasant. Procrastination is a natural response when faced with difficult or uncertain tasks, but it can significantly hinder progress and lead to feelings of frustration and guilt.

Another major internal challenge is self-doubt. Doubting your abilities can lead to a lack of confidence and make it difficult to take consistent action toward your goals. People often wonder if they can achieve their goals, which can lead to hesitation or quitting when things get tough.

External distractions are another common obstacle that disrupts discipline. In today's hyper-connected world, constant notifications from smartphones, emails, and social media can quickly derail focus and productivity. While these distractions may seem harmless in the moment, they can cumulatively have a significant impact on your ability to maintain consistent progress toward long-term goals.

By identifying these common obstacles—whether they are internal or external—you can begin to develop strategies to manage and overcome them. Maintaining discipline and staying committed to your goals begins with understanding that these challenges are normal and addressable.

Strategies for Overcoming Procrastination

Procrastination is often one of the biggest barriers to staying committed, and overcoming it requires both self-awareness and the implementation of effective strategies. Procrastination often stems from fear of failure, perfectionism, or simply feeling overwhelmed by the size or complexity of a task.

One of the most effective strategies for overcoming procrastination is breaking tasks down into smaller steps. When a project feels overwhelming, breaking it into manageable, bite-sized pieces can make it easier to get started. For instance, instead of focusing on writing an entire report, break it down into sections—such as brainstorming, outlining, drafting, and editing. This approach reduces the mental burden and makes the task feel more achievable.

Another powerful tool for combatting procrastination is the two-minute rule. If a task takes less than two minutes to complete, do it immediately. This helps eliminate small tasks that often pile up and cause stress. Additionally, starting with small, straightforward tasks can build momentum and make it easier to transition into more complex or challenging tasks.

Timeboxing is another proven method for overcoming procrastination. By setting a specific amount of time to work on a task—such as 25 or 30 minutes, followed by a short break—you create a sense of urgency that reduces the temptation to procrastinate. The Pomodoro Technique, which utilizes this method, can be particularly effective in maintaining focus and making consistent progress on tasks.

Finally, developing self-compassion is crucial for overcoming procrastination. People often procrastinate because they fear failure or are overly self-critical. By practicing self-compassion and accepting that mistakes are part of the learning process, you can reduce the fear that fuels procrastination and become more willing to take action despite uncertainties.

Dealing with Self-Doubt and Fear of Failure

Self-doubt and fear of failure are internal obstacles that can significantly undermine discipline and derail progress. The fear of failing often prevents individuals from taking action or pursuing their goals with confidence, while self-doubt erodes the belief that success is attainable. Both of these challenges require a shift in mindset and the cultivation of resilience.

One of the most effective ways to combat self-doubt is by building self-efficacy. Self-efficacy refers to your belief in your ability to succeed in specific situations or accomplish tasks. To build self-efficacy, start by setting small, achievable goals that allow you to experience success. Each success, no matter how small, reinforces your confidence and builds momentum toward larger accomplishments.

Reframing failure is another important strategy. Instead of viewing failure as a reflection of your abilities or potential, see it as a learning opportunity. Every failure offers valuable lessons that can help you refine your approach and improve future efforts. When you adopt a growth mindset—understanding that abilities can be developed through effort and learning—you become less fearful of failure and more willing to take risks that can lead to long-term success.

Visualizing success is another technique to overcome self-doubt. Visualization involves imagining yourself successfully achieving your goals and navigating challenges with confidence. This mental rehearsal can help reduce anxiety and reinforce positive beliefs about your capabilities. By consistently visualizing positive outcomes, you begin to internalize the belief that you are capable of overcoming obstacles and achieving success.

Finally, surrounding yourself with a supportive community can help combat self-doubt and fear of failure. Trusted friends, mentors, or accountability partners can provide encouragement and perspective during difficult times. They can help remind you of your strengths, challenge negative self-talk, and offer constructive feedback that helps you stay committed to your goals.

Managing External Distractions

External distractions can derail even the most disciplined individuals, particularly in today's digital age. Constant interruptions from notifications, social media, emails, and other external stimuli can make it difficult to stay focused on your goals. To maintain discipline in the face of distractions, it's essential to create an environment that minimizes these interruptions and supports deep work.

One of the most effective ways to manage distractions is by setting boundaries. This could involve turning off non-essential notifications during work hours, establishing "do not disturb" periods, or creating a distraction-free zone in your workspace. By minimizing the number of interruptions in your environment, you can maintain focus and discipline for longer periods of time.

Another useful strategy is batch processing. Rather than constantly checking your email, social media, or phone throughout the day, set specific times to handle these tasks in bulk. For example, you might choose to check your email at 11 AM and 3 PM instead of every time a notification pops up. This approach allows you to stay focused on important tasks without being derailed by minor distractions.

Practicing digital detox can also help. Scheduling periods of time—such as one day a week or certain hours of the day—where you completely disconnect from technology can help reset your focus and prevent burnout. These breaks from the constant influx of information allow your mind to rest, making it easier to stay disciplined when you return to your tasks.

Finally, using productivity tools and apps can help manage distractions. Apps like RescueTime or Focus@Will can track how you're spending your time and help you stay on task by blocking distracting websites or providing background noise conducive to concentration. These tools can provide an extra layer of accountability and support as you work toward maintaining discipline.

Building Resilience in the Face of Setbacks

Setbacks are inevitable on the journey toward long-term success, but resilience—the ability to bounce back from challenges—determines whether you stay committed or give up. Developing a mindset that perceives obstacles as temporary challenges that you can overcome with effort and persistence is essential for building resilience.

One of the most important aspects of resilience is reframing setbacks as opportunities for growth. When you encounter an obstacle, rather than seeing it as a failure, ask yourself, "What can I learn from this experience?" This shift in perspective allows you to approach challenges with curiosity and problem-solving, rather than frustration or defeat.

Self-compassion is another key component of resilience. It's easy to be harsh on yourself after a setback, but self-criticism often leads to feelings of inadequacy and discouragement. Instead, practice self-compassion by treating yourself with the same kindness and understanding you would offer a friend. Acknowledging that setbacks are a normal part of the process helps you stay motivated and focused on the bigger picture.

Developing emotional regulation skills is also crucial for building resilience. When setbacks occur, it's important to manage the emotions that arise—whether it's frustration, anger, or disappointment—so that they don't derail your progress. Techniques such as deep breathing, meditation, or journaling can help regulate these emotions, allowing you to process them and refocus on your goals.

Finally, building resilience involves having a long-term perspective. Realizing that success is a journey, not a race, enables you to overcome temporary obstacles without losing sight of your ultimate objective. By staying committed to the bigger picture and viewing setbacks as part of the journey, you can maintain the discipline needed to push through challenges and continue progressing.

The Importance of Accountability Systems

Accountability is a powerful tool for maintaining discipline and overcoming obstacles. When you hold yourself accountable—or better yet, involve others in holding you accountable—you create an additional layer of commitment that makes it more difficult to stray from your goals. Accountability systems can take many forms, from personal tracking methods to involving friends, colleagues, or mentors in your progress.

One simple but effective accountability strategy is to track your progress. This could be as straightforward as checking off tasks on a daily to-do list, keeping a journal of your accomplishments, or using a habit-tracking app. Having a visual representation of your progress can serve as a powerful motivator and reminder of your commitment.

Another highly effective method is to establish an accountability partner. This could be a friend, colleague, or mentor who is also working toward their own goals. You can regularly check in with each other, share your progress, and offer mutual support and encouragement. Knowing that someone else is expecting you to report on your progress creates a sense of responsibility that makes it harder to procrastinate or give up. Accountability partners help provide perspective during setbacks and celebrate milestones together, reinforcing a positive and disciplined approach to goal achievement.

In addition to accountability partners, you might consider joining or creating an accountability group. These groups consist of individuals who meet regularly (in person or virtually) to discuss their goals, challenges, and progress. Group accountability can be particularly powerful because it provides a sense of community and support. Group members often offer insights, feedback, and encouragement that help maintain motivation and discipline over the long term.

A more formalized approach to accountability is working with a coach or mentor. Mentors can offer guidance based on their experiences, helping you navigate obstacles with greater clarity and confidence. They hold you accountable by providing regular feedback and helping you stay on track, even when things become tough. A coach or mentor often provides both structure and motivation, which can be invaluable for staying disciplined through challenging times.

Accountability systems also work well when combined with rewards and consequences. Setting specific rewards for achieving milestones (such as treating yourself to something special when a major task is completed) creates a positive reinforcement loop. Conversely, implementing small consequences for missed deadlines or uncompleted tasks can add an extra layer of motivation to stay disciplined. These consequences don't need to be punitive; they could be as simple as a donation to a cause you support or reframing your work schedule to make up for lost time.

Ultimately, accountability systems create external structures that support internal discipline. Relying on both personal tracking methods and external accountability from others positions you for long-term success, even during challenging times.

Maintaining Momentum and Avoiding Burnout

Maintaining momentum is crucial for long-term discipline. Even with the best plans and systems in place, there will be times when motivation dips or progress slows. The key is to avoid losing momentum entirely and to prevent burnout, which can quickly derail progress.

One of the most effective ways to maintain momentum is by focusing on small, consistent wins. When you're working toward a large, long-term goal, it's easy to feel overwhelmed or discouraged by the distance between where you are and where you want to be. Breaking down larger goals into smaller, more manageable tasks allows you to celebrate frequent victories, which keeps your motivation high and reinforces the discipline needed to stay committed.

Regularly evaluating your progress can also help you maintain momentum. Take time to reflect on what's working and what's not, and adjust your approach as needed. This allows you to stay flexible and avoid frustration if you encounter obstacles or slowdowns. The key is to stay focused on the bigger picture and remain patient as you navigate setbacks.

Another essential factor in maintaining momentum is pacing yourself to avoid burnout. Burnout occurs when individuals push themselves too hard without adequate rest or balance, leading to mental, physical, and emotional exhaustion. To avoid burnout, it's important to build regular breaks and downtime into your schedule. This could mean taking a day off after completing a major task or making sure you get enough sleep and engage in activities that recharge your energy.

Self-care is an integral part of maintaining discipline. Far from being a luxury, self-care practices—such as exercise, meditation, hobbies, or spending time with loved ones—help prevent burnout and maintain long-term productivity. By taking care of your physical and mental health, you ensure that you have the energy and focus needed to stay disciplined over time.

Finally, don't underestimate the importance of celebrating progress. Even if you haven't reached your ultimate goal, recognizing how far you've come can provide a sense of accomplishment and motivation to keep going. Small celebrations—such as acknowledging the completion of a major milestone or rewarding yourself for maintaining discipline over time—reinforce the positive habits and mindsets that lead to long-term success.

Building a Supportive Environment

Your environment plays a key role in your ability to overcome obstacles and stay committed to your goals. A supportive environment helps reduce distractions, minimize friction, and reinforce discipline. Building such an environment involves both your physical space and the people you surround yourself with.

Start by creating a dedicated workspace that promotes focus and minimizes distractions. Whether it's a home office, a quiet corner of a room, or a co-working space, having a specific area dedicated to your work can improve productivity and reinforce discipline. Keep your workspace organized and free from unnecessary clutter, which can add to cognitive overload and decrease focus.

In addition to organizing your physical environment, consider how you can optimize your digital environment to support discipline. For example, you might use apps that block distracting websites during work hours, disable non-essential notifications on your phone, or schedule regular digital detoxes to minimize information overload. These strategies reduce the temptation to engage in time-wasting activities and help you stay focused on your priorities.

Beyond your immediate surroundings, the people in your life also contribute to a supportive environment. Surrounding yourself with individuals who share similar goals or values can provide encouragement, accountability, and inspiration. Whether it's a partner, friend, mentor, or peer group, having people who understand your journey and offer support can make it easier to stay disciplined when challenges arise.

Conversely, it's important to point out when certain relationships or environments are counterproductive to your goals. Toxic environments—whether it's negative relationships, unsupportive peers, or work cultures that promote burnout—can undermine your discipline and lead to setbacks. Part of building a supportive environment involves setting boundaries and, when necessary, removing yourself from situations that detract from your progress.

Creating an environment that nurtures discipline and long-term success requires intentionality. By optimizing your physical and digital spaces and surrounding yourself with supportive individuals, you create a foundation that helps sustain your commitment, even during difficult times.

Embracing a Growth Mindset

Adopting a growth mindset is one of the most powerful tools for overcoming obstacles and staying committed to long-term goals. A growth mindset, a concept popularized by psychologist Carol Dweck, refers to the belief that abilities and intelligence can be developed through effort, learning, and persistence. In contrast, a fixed mindset believes that abilities are innate and unchangeable.

Embracing a growth mindset is essential for overcoming challenges because it allows you to view obstacles as opportunities for growth rather than as insurmountable roadblocks. Individuals with a growth mindset are more likely to persist in the face of setbacks, seek feedback, and continuously improve their skills. This mindset fosters resilience and discipline, as it encourages a proactive approach to challenges.

One way to cultivate a growth mindset is to focus on the process, not just the outcome. Instead of obsessing over whether you've achieved your goal, pay attention to the steps you're taking and the effort you're putting in. By valuing the journey as much as the destination, you become less discouraged by setbacks and more motivated by incremental progress.

Reframing failure as a learning experience is another crucial aspect of the growth mindset. When faced with failure, individuals with a growth mindset ask themselves, "What can I learn from this?" rather than viewing failure as a personal shortcoming. This mindset shift enables you to bounce back more quickly from mistakes and continue moving forward with renewed motivation.

Finally, adopting a growth mindset requires practicing self-compassion. Discipline does not mean perfection, and it's important to allow yourself the space to make mistakes and learn from them. By being kind to yourself and embracing the idea that growth takes time, you'll be better equipped to handle challenges and stay committed to your long-term goals.

Staying Committed to the Long Journey

The journey toward mastering discipline and achieving long-term success is rarely straightforward. Obstacles such as procrastination, self-doubt, fear of failure, distractions, and setbacks are inevitable. However, by developing resilience, implementing effective accountability systems, creating supportive environments, and embracing a growth mindset, you can overcome these challenges and stay committed to your goals.

Remember, discipline is a skill that grows stronger with consistent effort and practice. While setbacks may occur, each challenge you overcome strengthens your ability to stay focused and dedicated. By maintaining your commitment to long-term success, you ensure that the obstacles along the way become stepping stones rather than roadblocks.

Stay patient, trust the process, and remain disciplined—success is the result of sustained effort over time. With the right strategies and mindset, you can overcome any obstacle and continue moving forward on the path to your greatest achievements.

Chapter 7

The Impact of Discipline on Personal and Professional Growth

Discipline in Personal Development

Discipline is one of the most critical factors in personal growth. Personal development encompasses a wide range of goals, from improving physical health to building emotional intelligence, learning new skills, or pursuing hobbies that bring joy and fulfillment. Whatever the objective, discipline is the vehicle that enables sustained progress and improvement.

At the heart of personal development is the concept of consistency. Without consistency, even the most ambitious self-improvement goals remain unrealized. Discipline ensures that actions toward personal development are taken regularly, turning aspirations into tangible habits and long-term results. For example, someone who wants to improve their physical health must consistently exercise and maintain a balanced diet. Without discipline, it's easy to fall back into unhealthy habits, but with a disciplined mindset, even challenging routines can become sustainable over time.

Discipline also drives the development of emotional intelligence. Building emotional resilience—such as learning to manage stress, control impulsive reactions, and maintain healthy relationships—requires continual self-awareness and intentional effort. When you apply discipline to emotional growth, you become better equipped to handle life's inevitable ups and downs with a calm and balanced approach.

Another important aspect of discipline in personal development is the process of learning new skills. Whether you're learning a new language, mastering a musical instrument, or expanding your professional expertise, skill development requires time and sustained effort. Discipline ensures that you consistently practice and engage with the learning process, even when progress feels slow or challenging. Over time, these small efforts compound, leading to mastery.

Discipline also fosters self-confidence. As you build disciplined habits and see the results of your efforts, you develop greater trust in your abilities and your capacity for growth. This sense of confidence enhances your willingness to take on new challenges, expand your comfort zone, and continue striving for self-improvement.

Finally, discipline provides a sense of purpose and fulfillment in personal development. When you commit to a personal growth journey and consistently take steps to improve, you cultivate a deeper connection to your values and long-term vision. This alignment between daily actions and long-term aspirations creates a sense of meaning and satisfaction that enriches your life.

Discipline in Physical and Mental Health

Discipline is integral to maintaining and improving both physical and mental health. Consistently adhering to healthy habits—such as regular exercise, balanced nutrition, proper sleep, and stress management—requires discipline, but the rewards are significant. Physical health improves, energy levels rise, and mental clarity is enhanced, all of which contribute to greater well-being.

Exercise is one of the most common areas where discipline is required. Many people set goals to improve their fitness or health, but sticking to an exercise routine can be challenging. Discipline helps you push through moments of resistance, allowing you to make exercise a regular part of your life. The long-term benefits of disciplined physical activity are well-documented: better cardiovascular health, stronger muscles and bones, enhanced mental health, and increased longevity.

Nutrition is another area where discipline plays a vital role. In a world filled with processed foods and instant gratification, maintaining a balanced, healthy diet requires consistent effort. Whether it's meal planning, resisting the temptation of unhealthy snacks, or ensuring that your body receives the nutrients it needs, discipline ensures that you make choices aligned with long-term health goals.

Mental health also benefits from discipline. Practices such as meditation, mindfulness, or journaling require consistency to yield results, but these habits can dramatically improve mental clarity, reduce stress, and enhance emotional well-being. Regularly engaging in these practices builds mental resilience, making it easier to manage life's challenges with a calm and composed mind.

Moreover, discipline is crucial when seeking help for mental health challenges. Attending therapy sessions regularly, following treatment plans, or engaging in activities that support mental health (such as connecting with supportive communities) often requires sustained effort. Those who approach mental health with a disciplined mindset are more likely to see progress and long-term improvements.

Ultimately, discipline in health involves making daily decisions that promote your overall well-being, even when it may be easier to choose the easiest path. The cumulative effect of disciplined actions leads to a healthier, more balanced, and more fulfilling life.

Discipline in Lifelong Learning

Lifelong learning is an essential component of personal and professional growth, and discipline is the driving force behind it. In today's rapidly evolving world, where new information and technologies emerge constantly, the ability to learn continuously is a key differentiator for success. Discipline ensures that you remain committed to learning, even when it's challenging or inconvenient.

Curiosity—the desire to learn more about the world—is a key part of lifelong learning. Discipline enhances this curiosity by ensuring that you consistently seek out new information, acquire new skills, and expand your knowledge base. Whether it's enrolling in online courses, reading books, attending workshops, or learning from mentors, disciplined learners are those who prioritize growth over comfort.

Discipline also helps manage the time and effort required to learn effectively. Learning something new often requires sustained focus and practice. For example, learning a new language involves regular practice, memorization, and application. Without discipline, it's simple to lose motivation or become distracted by other priorities. However, with a disciplined approach, you can dedicate specific time to learning, ensuring steady progress over time.

Moreover, discipline supports more profound learning. Surface-level understanding may come quickly, but mastering a subject or skill requires a commitment to ongoing education and practice. By applying discipline, learners move beyond the basics and dive into advanced concepts, fostering expertise in their chosen field or area of interest.

Another important element of lifelong learning is applying the knowledge you've gained. Discipline ensures that you acquire new information and find ways to integrate it into your life or career. Applying your learning reinforces its retention and propels meaningful progress.

Lifelong learning requires resilience because there will inevitably be moments of frustration, confusion, or slow progress. Discipline ensures that you continue to learn even in the face of these challenges, developing a mindset that embraces learning as a continuous and rewarding journey.

Discipline in Career Advancement

Discipline is a critical factor in professional growth and career advancement. Whether you're aiming for a promotion, seeking new opportunities, or striving to become a leader in your field, consistent effort and a disciplined approach are essential to achieving career success. While talent and education can provide opportunities, discipline is the key to sustaining progress and achieving upward mobility in the workplace.

At the core of career discipline is the ability to consistently deliver results. Professionals who maintain discipline in their work are those who meet deadlines, exceed expectations, and demonstrate reliability. Employers and colleagues value individuals who can consistently perform at a high level because they are dependable and trustworthy. This consistency, driven by discipline, makes it easier to build a reputation for excellence and professionalism.

Discipline also plays a key role in developing the skills necessary for career advancement. In a fast-changing job market, staying relevant often requires acquiring new skills and adapting to emerging trends. Whether it's learning a new software program, developing leadership skills, or staying informed about industry developments, discipline ensures that you invest in your professional growth on a consistent basis.

Moreover, disciplined individuals are often better at managing their time and responsibilities, which allows them to handle increased workloads and more complex tasks. As responsibilities grow in a professional setting, the ability to prioritize, stay organized, and remain focused becomes essential. Discipline ensures that you can balance competing demands while maintaining a high standard of work.

In addition to fostering skill development and productivity, discipline helps professionals manage the obstacles and setbacks that inevitably arise in their careers. Career advancement is rarely linear—there will be times of frustration, failure, or stagnation. Disciplined individuals are able to maintain their focus, continue putting in the necessary effort, and view these setbacks as temporary obstacles, not permanent roadblocks.

This resilience is often the key differentiator between those who succeed in their careers and those who plateau.

Lastly, discipline fosters leadership. Leaders are expected to be role models for others, demonstrating commitment, accountability, and excellence. A disciplined leader inspires their team through action, showing that hard work, consistency, and dedication lead to success. By embodying these qualities, you can rise to leadership positions and inspire others to achieve their potential.

Discipline in Entrepreneurship

For entrepreneurs, discipline is one of the most valuable skills. Starting and growing a business requires a relentless focus on long-term goals, the ability to manage uncertainty, and the willingness to put in consistent effort over an extended period. Without discipline, it's simple for entrepreneurs to become overwhelmed by the challenges of building a business or to lose focus on the actions that drive success.

One of the primary ways discipline supports entrepreneurship is by helping entrepreneurs maintain focus on their core mission. Entrepreneurs frequently assume multiple roles such as sales, marketing, operations, and product development, and the numerous tasks vying for their attention can easily distract them. Discipline helps prioritize the most important actions that move the business forward, ensuring that energy is directed toward high-impact activities.

Discipline is also critical for financial management, a key component of entrepreneurial success. Managing cash flow, controlling expenses, and investing in the right opportunities require careful planning and restraint. Entrepreneurs who lack financial discipline may overspend, take unnecessary risks, or neglect important investments. On the other hand, disciplined financial management helps ensure long-term stability and growth.

Entrepreneurs also benefit from discipline when it comes to decision-making. The entrepreneurial journey is filled with uncertainty, and it can be tempting to make impulsive decisions based on short-term opportunities. However, disciplined entrepreneurs take a long-term view, evaluating each decision carefully before taking action. They resist the urge to chase every opportunity and instead focus on what aligns with their overall mission and goals. This disciplined approach to decision-making ensures that entrepreneurs remain strategic, minimizing risks while maximizing long-term potential.

Time management is another area where discipline plays a pivotal role in entrepreneurship. Entrepreneurs often work long hours, balancing multiple responsibilities, and it can be tempting to work on everything at once. However, without discipline, entrepreneurs may waste time on low-value tasks or distractions that don't contribute to the growth of their business. Disciplined entrepreneurs prioritize their time effectively, focusing on tasks that drive revenue, enhance customer satisfaction, or improve product development.

Discipline also fosters resilience in entrepreneurship. Building a business is challenging, and setbacks are inevitable. Entrepreneurs who cultivate discipline are better equipped to persevere through difficult times. Instead of giving up when they face obstacles, disciplined entrepreneurs maintain their focus, adjust their strategies, and continue to work toward their goals. This perseverance is often what separates successful entrepreneurs from those who fail.

Finally, discipline is essential for maintaining work-life balance as an entrepreneur. The pressures of running a business can lead to burnout if not managed properly. Entrepreneurs who apply discipline to their personal lives—ensuring they take time for rest, relaxation, and family—are more likely to sustain their energy and passion for the business over the long term. By creating boundaries and adhering to structured routines, entrepreneurs can enjoy both personal fulfillment and professional success.

Discipline in Leadership and Team Building

Leadership requires discipline, both in personal conduct and in the way a leader manages and motivates a team. A disciplined leader sets an example by consistently demonstrating commitment, reliability, and accountability. In turn, this fosters a culture of discipline within the team, where each member feels responsible for their contributions to the overall mission.

One of the key ways that discipline manifests in leadership is through leading by example. A disciplined leader shows up on time, meets deadlines, and upholds the standards they expect from their team. This consistency builds trust and respect, as team members see the leader as someone who not only talks about discipline but practices it as well. In this way, discipline becomes contagious, inspiring others to adopt similar behaviors.

Discipline is also crucial for setting and maintaining clear goals within a team. A leader's ability to define clear, actionable objectives for their team members ensures that everyone understands what is expected of them and how their efforts contribute to the broader organizational goals. Discipline ensures that these goals are regularly revisited and that progress is tracked, preventing drift and keeping the team aligned with its mission.

Additionally, discipline helps leaders maintain focus and priorities within their teams. In a fast-paced work environment, it's easy to become reactive, jumping from one crisis to the next. However, disciplined leaders maintain their focus on long-term objectives and avoid succumbing to excessive distractions. Disciplined leaders keep their teams focused on high-impact tasks and steer clear of unnecessary distractions.

Leaders demonstrate discipline in team building by holding themselves and their teams accountable. A disciplined leader ensures that team members are held to high standards and that they follow through on their commitments. This accountability creates a culture of ownership, where everyone understands the importance of their role and feels motivated to deliver results.

Moreover, discipline in leadership extends to managing conflict and providing feedback. Leaders who practice discipline in their communication are able to address challenges or conflicts with clarity, fairness, and professionalism. Instead of avoiding difficult conversations or reacting impulsively, disciplined leaders approach these situations with a balanced mindset, ensuring that issues are resolved constructively.

In summary, discipline in leadership not only improves personal effectiveness but also enhances team performance. By fostering a culture of accountability, clarity, and focus, disciplined leaders build teams that are aligned, motivated, and committed to achieving shared goals.

The Long-Term Benefits of Discipline in Professional Growth

Discipline is a key factor in achieving sustained professional growth. Whether you're looking to advance in your current role, switch careers, or become a leader in your field, the long-term benefits of discipline cannot be overstated. Professionals who apply discipline to their work consistently demonstrate reliability, resilience, and a willingness to learn and improve.

One of the most significant long-term benefits of discipline is reputation building. A strong reputation for reliability and excellence in any professional field provides access to new opportunities. Colleagues, supervisors, and industry peers respect and trust individuals who consistently deliver results, meet deadlines, and uphold high standards. Over time, this reputation becomes an invaluable asset, leading to career advancements, promotions, and leadership opportunities.

Discipline also fosters continuous improvement. In a world where industries are constantly evolving, staying relevant and competitive requires a commitment to learning and adaptation. Disciplined professionals invest in their personal and professional growth by regularly acquiring new skills, seeking feedback, and setting long-term career goals. This commitment to improvement ensures that they remain valuable contributors to their organizations and industries.

Additionally, disciplined professionals are often more adept at managing work-life balance. They understand the importance of boundaries, time management, and self-care, which helps prevent burnout and ensures long-term career sustainability. By creating healthy routines and habits, disciplined individuals maintain high levels of productivity without sacrificing personal well-being.

Another important benefit of discipline is resilience in the face of challenges. The ability to stay focused and motivated during difficult times is a hallmark of disciplined professionals. Whether it's navigating economic downturns, company restructuring, or personal setbacks, disciplined individuals are able to maintain their composure, adjust their strategies, and continue working toward their goals. This resilience helps them weather tough times and positions them as leaders who can guide others through adversity.

Finally, discipline helps professionals achieve financial stability and success. By consistently managing finances, setting clear financial goals, and practicing restraint in spending, disciplined individuals are more likely to build wealth and achieve financial independence over time. Whether it's saving for retirement, investing wisely, or making smart career decisions, financial discipline is a key driver of long-term success.

The Transformative Power of Discipline in Growth

In both personal and professional realms, discipline is a transformative force that unlocks new levels of achievement and fulfillment. From improving physical and mental health to advancing in your career or becoming a more effective leader, the benefits of discipline are profound and far-reaching. Discipline allows you to develop new skills, build strong relationships, overcome obstacles, and eventually achieve long-term success.

By cultivating discipline, you improve your daily habits and routines and create a foundation for sustained growth and resilience. Whether in your personal development, health, career, or relationships, discipline enables you to stay focused on what matters most and consistently take actions that move you closer to your goals.

The impact of discipline on personal and professional growth is not limited to individual success—it extends to your ability to inspire and lead others, create lasting change, and contribute meaningfully to your community and profession. A life filled with purpose, achievement, and fulfillment becomes possible when you embrace discipline as a core value.

Chapter 8

The Long Road to Success

More Stories of Discipline in Action

The Power of Real-World Examples

Throughout history, countless individuals have demonstrated the power of discipline in overcoming challenges and achieving long-term success. From world-renowned athletes to influential business leaders and creative visionaries, these stories provide living proof that discipline is the cornerstone of achievement. In this chapter, we'll explore several real-life examples of individuals who embraced discipline as the foundation for their success. These case studies will inspire and highlight the specific ways in which discipline enabled them to stay committed, persevere through setbacks, and ultimately reach their goals.

The road to success is rarely a straight path. It is so often filled with obstacles, failures, and moments of doubt. However, those who practice discipline consistently are able to navigate these challenges and keep their focus on their long-term vision. Let's take a look at some of the most compelling stories of discipline in action.

Case Study 1: Elon Musk—The Discipline of Vision and Work Ethic

Elon Musk, the CEO of Tesla and SpaceX, is widely recognized for his relentless work ethic, innovation, and ability to push the boundaries of what's possible. But what many may not fully appreciate is the extraordinary discipline that underpins Musk's success. His discipline is not just in his work habits but in his ability to maintain focus on audacious long-term goals, even in the face of seemingly insurmountable challenges.

Musk's journey to success was far from smooth. Both Tesla and SpaceX faced multiple moments of potential collapse. In 2008, SpaceX was on the verge of bankruptcy after three consecutive failed launches. At the same time, Tesla was struggling financially, and many predicted it wouldn't survive the global financial crisis. Yet Musk's discipline and unwavering belief in his vision for the future of electric vehicles and space exploration kept him focused.

Musk's ability to balance time between two high-stakes companies—Tesla and SpaceX—demonstrates a level of discipline in managing not only his workload but also his mental and physical energy. Musk is known for working 80 to 100 hours a week, carefully structuring his time to ensure that both companies continue to innovate and succeed. His intense focus on productivity and his disciplined approach to work have been key to his ability to achieve breakthroughs in industries that many believed were impossible to revolutionize.

Moreover, Musk's discipline extends to his financial management. At a time when both Tesla and SpaceX were struggling, Musk made the disciplined decision to invest his own money into keeping them afloat, even though it meant risking his personal fortune. His decision to maintain this discipline in financial commitment, despite the risks, eventually paid off as both companies became successful.

Musk's story illustrates that discipline is about more than just hard work—it's about the consistent application of focus, resilience, and strategic thinking over time. His unwavering commitment to long-term goals, even in the face of adversity, exemplifies the strength of staying committed to a vision.

Case Study 2: Serena Williams—The Discipline of Practice and Mental Resilience

Serena Williams, one of the greatest tennis players of all time, is a perfect example of how discipline in practice, physical conditioning, and mental resilience can lead to unparalleled success. Williams' career, which includes 23 Grand Slam singles titles, was built on an extraordinary level of discipline that began in her childhood and continued throughout her decades-long career.

From an early age, Williams developed the habit of disciplined practice, often spending hours on the court with her father and sister, Venus, perfecting her technique and building her strength. Her rigorous training routines were designed not only to improve her skills but also to cultivate the mental toughness required to compete at the highest levels of the sport. Williams' ability to maintain discipline in her training, even at the peak of her performance, significantly contributed to her longevity as an athlete.

In addition to physical discipline, Williams developed an extraordinary level of mental resilience. Tennis, like many sports, is as much a mental game as a physical one. Over the years,

Williams faced numerous setbacks, including injuries, personal challenges, and media scrutiny. However, her disciplined mindset allowed her to stay focused on her goals, push through adversity, and continue competing at an elite level.

One of the most inspiring aspects of Williams' story is her comeback after pregnancy. Many athletes struggle to return to peak form after taking time off, but Williams approached her comeback with the same level of discipline and determination that had defined her career. She focused on rebuilding her strength, managing her health, and mentally preparing for the challenges ahead.

Williams' disciplined approach to both physical and mental preparation has been a defining factor in her success. Her story demonstrates that talent alone is not enough; it is the discipline to practice, to persevere, and to stay mentally resilient that leads to sustained excellence.

Case Study 3: J.K. Rowling—The Discipline of Persistence in the Face of Rejection

J.K. Rowling, the creator of the Harry Potter series, exemplifies how discipline and persistence can transform rejection into triumph. Before becoming one of the world's most successful authors, Rowling faced numerous challenges, including financial hardship, personal struggles, and repeated rejections from publishers. However, her discipline in writing and her refusal to give up on her dream eventually led to unprecedented success.

Rowling began writing the first Harry Potter book while struggling as a single mother, living on government assistance. Despite her difficult circumstances, she maintained a disciplined writing schedule, often working in coffee shops with her infant daughter by her side. Her commitment to writing every day, even when faced with the pressures of daily life, exemplifies the discipline required to complete a long-term creative project.

After finishing the manuscript for Harry Potter and the Philosopher's Stone, Rowling faced a string of rejections from publishers. Over the course of a year, her book was rejected by twelve publishers, many of whom doubted that a story about a young wizard would have commercial appeal. However, Rowling's disciplined mindset allowed her to persevere. She continued to submit her manuscript, believing in its potential despite the repeated setbacks.

Rowling's discipline paid off when Bloomsbury Publishing finally accepted her manuscript. The Harry Potter series went on to become one of the best-selling book series of all time, and Rowling herself became a billionaire and a global literary icon. Her story is a powerful reminder that discipline is often the key to success in the face of rejection. By staying committed to her craft and refusing to let setbacks define her, Rowling was able to achieve her dream.

Case Study 4: Dwayne "The Rock" Johnson—The Discipline of Hard Work and Adaptability

Dwayne "The Rock" Johnson is known for his successful career as a professional wrestler, actor, and entrepreneur. Behind his impressive persona, a deeply ingrained sense of discipline has driven his diverse achievements. Johnson's journey from a failed football player to one of the highest-paid actors in Hollywood is a testament to his work ethic, adaptability, and constant search for success.

Johnson's early career was marked by setbacks. After a brief stint in professional football, Johnson's dreams of playing in the NFL were cut short due to injuries. At a low point in his life, he had only $7 to his name. However, instead of giving up, Johnson turned to professional wrestling, where he applied the same discipline that had defined his approach to sports. His relentless training, commitment to improving his performance, and disciplined work ethic helped him rise to fame in the WWE.

When Johnson transitioned from wrestling to acting, many doubted whether he could succeed in Hollywood. However, Johnson's adaptability and disciplined approach to his new career path allowed him to break through barriers. He took on a wide range of roles, from action heroes to comedic characters, all while maintaining his disciplined work ethic and focus on self-improvement.

Beyond his physical discipline, Johnson has shown a commitment to continuous learning and self-development. As an entrepreneur, he has launched several successful businesses, including his own production company and a tequila brand, demonstrating his ability to apply discipline across multiple ventures.

Johnson's story illustrates that discipline is not just about working hard—it's about staying adaptable, continuously improving, and being willing to embrace new opportunities. His disciplined mindset has allowed him to excel in multiple fields, from sports to entertainment to business.

Case Study 5: Malala Yousafzai—The Discipline of Courage and Advocacy

Malala Yousafzai, the youngest-ever recipient of the Nobel Peace Prize, is a powerful example of how discipline can drive social change. Malala's advocacy for girls' education began at a young age when she defied the Taliban's ban on education for girls in her native Pakistan. Her bravery and discipline in standing up for her beliefs, even in the face of danger, have inspired millions around the world.

Malala's journey was not easy. A Taliban gunman shot her in 2012 while she was riding the bus to school. Many people in her situation might have given up, but Malala's discipline, courage, and determination only grew stronger. After surviving the attack, she continued to advocate for girls' education on a global scale, using her platform to raise awareness and bring about real change.

Malala's disciplined approach to her advocacy involves a deep commitment to education, both for herself and for others. After recovering from her injuries, she continued her education while also working tirelessly to promote access to education for girls worldwide. She founded the Malala Fund, which supports education projects in countries affected by conflict and poverty.

Malala's story demonstrates that discipline is not just about achieving personal success—it's about using your determination and commitment to create meaningful change in the world. Her disciplined focus on her cause has allowed her to navigate immense challenges and remain unwavering in her mission to ensure that every girl is entitled to an education. Despite facing personal threats and physical harm, Malala's disciplined commitment to her advocacy has made her a global symbol of courage, perseverance, and resilience.

Malala's story is an inspiring reminder that discipline, when paired with a strong sense of purpose, can drive extraordinary social impact. She shows us that discipline is not only a tool for individual achievement but also a powerful force for collective progress and justice.

Case Study 6: Stephen King—The Discipline of Daily Writing and Creativity

Stephen King is one of the most prolific and successful authors of all time, known for his ability to consistently produce bestsellers in multiple genres, from horror to fantasy and beyond. His success is not simply the result of talent but of an extraordinary level of discipline that has allowed him to write more than 60 novels, dozens of short stories, and numerous works of nonfiction.

King's daily writing routine is a testament to his disciplined approach. He famously writes every single day, including holidays and birthdays, and aims to complete a specific word count before finishing his writing session. This discipline ensures that he maintains a constant flow of creative output, even on days when inspiration may be lacking. By committing to the practice of writing daily, King has turned creativity into a structured, repeatable process rather than waiting for inspiration to strike.

King's discipline extends beyond his writing schedule. He also emphasizes the importance of reading widely and constantly honing his craft. His ability to balance both writing and reading has allowed him to develop a profound understanding of storytelling and character development, which has contributed to the quality and diversity of his work.

King's career also demonstrates the importance of resilience in the face of setbacks. Early in his writing career, he faced numerous rejections from publishers, and his now-famous novel *Carrie* was initially rejected 30 times before finally being accepted for publication. King's disciplined persistence allowed him to overcome these rejections and continue writing, eventually leading to his breakthrough and subsequent success.

Stephen King's story illustrates the power of discipline in the creative process. By maintaining a disciplined approach to daily writing, he has been able to consistently produce high-quality work over several decades, making him one of the most accomplished authors in modern literature.

Case Study 7: Angela Duckworth—The Discipline of Grit and Perseverance

Angela Duckworth, a psychologist and author of the bestselling book *Grit: The Power of Passion and Perseverance,* has dedicated her career to studying the role of discipline in success. Through her research, Duckworth has shown that grit—a combination of passion and perseverance over the long term—is a key predictor of success, often more important than talent or intelligence. Her findings highlight the importance of disciplined effort in achieving long-term goals.

Duckworth's concept of grit is grounded in the idea that success is not about short-term bursts of effort but about sustained commitment to a goal over years or even decades. This sustained effort requires discipline, particularly when progress is slow, setbacks occur, or motivation wanes. Duckworth's research demonstrates that individuals with high levels of grit are more likely to succeed because they are able to maintain discipline over the long term.

One of the most powerful aspects of Duckworth's work is her emphasis on the importance of deliberate practice—the disciplined, focused effort to improve skills over time. Deliberate practice involves setting specific goals, seeking feedback, and consistently working to improve performance. This approach requires not only physical discipline but also mental discipline, as it often involves pushing through discomfort and frustration to achieve incremental progress.

Duckworth's own journey is a reflection of the principles she advocates. Her disciplined approach to her research and writing has made her a leading voice in the field of psychology, and her work has influenced educators, leaders, and individuals around the world to embrace the power of perseverance and discipline.

Angela Duckworth's story reminds us that success is not about natural ability alone but about the disciplined pursuit of excellence over time. Her research and personal journey demonstrate that with enough grit, passion, and discipline, individuals can achieve remarkable things, regardless of the obstacles they face.

Lessons Learned from Stories of Discipline

The stories of Elon Musk, Serena Williams, J.K. Rowling, Dwayne "The Rock" Johnson, Malala Yousafzai, Stephen King, and Angela Duckworth provide compelling examples of how discipline can drive extraordinary success across a wide range of fields. These individuals, whether in business, sports, literature, advocacy, or creativity, all share a deep commitment to discipline, perseverance, and long-term goals.

From these case studies, several key lessons emerge:

Discipline Creates Consistency

These people succeeded because they showed up every day and worked diligently even when they faced challenges, failures, or lack of motivation.

Resilience is key

Discipline allows people to bounce back from setbacks, rejections, and failures. Success is not a straight path, and those who achieve their goals are often those who can remain disciplined through adversity.

Long-Term Focus

The individuals in these stories maintained a long-term perspective, understanding that success often requires years of effort and discipline. They resisted the temptation of instant gratification and stayed committed to their vision.

Mental and Physical Discipline

Success requires both mental and physical discipline. Whether it's maintaining focus, managing time effectively, or sticking to rigorous training schedules, discipline in all aspects of life is necessary to achieve lasting success.

The Power of Purpose

Maintaining discipline becomes easier when it aligns with a broader purpose or passion. Each of these individuals had a clear vision or goal that motivated their disciplined efforts, which made it easier for them to remain committed even when facing difficulties.

In the end, these stories of discipline in action serve as powerful reminders that success is not solely determined by talent; rather, it depends on the ability to remain disciplined, focused, and resilient over the long term. By applying the lessons from these individuals to our lives, we can develop the discipline necessary to achieve our own goals, no matter how ambitious they may be.

Chapter 9

Building a Legacy Through Discipline

Defining Legacy

A legacy is what remains of a person's lifelong work long after they are gone. It is the lasting impact that an individual has on others, their community, or even the world at large. Legacies are often thought of in terms of wealth or tangible accomplishments, but a true legacy is about much more than material success. It's about the values, lessons, and influence that shape future generations.

The building of a meaningful legacy is not accidental; it requires intentionality, sustained effort, and, most importantly, discipline. While talent, opportunity, and vision are certainly factors in how one makes an impact on the world, discipline is what allows individuals to continually refine their craft, push through setbacks, and create something that endures beyond their lifetime. Without discipline, even the most ambitious goals are likely to remain unrealized.

In this chapter, we'll explore how discipline plays a fundamental role in building a legacy. Whether it's through leadership, innovation, community service, or creative contributions, discipline is the thread that weaves a person's work into a lasting, meaningful impact. By examining the stories of those who have left enduring legacies, we'll see that disciplined action is not only key to personal success but also to creating a positive and lasting influence on the world.

Discipline in Leadership and Influence

Leadership is one of the most powerful ways to build a legacy, and discipline is a core quality of effective leaders. Whether they are leading a company, a country, or a movement, outstanding leaders are those who are able to maintain focus on long-term goals, inspire others to follow their vision, and persist in the face of challenges. The legacies of leaders like Mahatma Gandhi, Nelson Mandela, and Martin Luther King Jr. were not built overnight; they were the result of years of disciplined effort and unwavering commitment to their causes.

Leaders with discipline are able to navigate the complex challenges of leadership with resilience and consistency. They don't give in to short-term pressures or distractions; instead, they remain focused on the bigger picture and their long-term mission. This ability to stay the course, even when things are difficult or uncertain, is what allows leaders to build legacies that endure. Their disciplined approach to decision-making and problem-solving ensures that their contributions are not fleeting but have a lasting impact.

A key component of disciplined leadership is the ability to foster discipline within the teams or communities they lead. Leaders who practice discipline set a standard for others to follow, creating a culture of accountability, excellence, and continuous improvement. This ripple effect of discipline ensures that the leader's influence extends beyond their immediate actions and continues to shape the values and behaviors of those who follow in their footsteps.

Moreover, disciplined leaders are often able to balance short-term demands with long-term goals. Their ability to balance immediate challenges with long-term goals enables them to establish sustainable organizations or movements that endure long after their departure. Discipline in leadership plays a crucial role in establishing a lasting legacy.

Discipline in Innovation and Creativity

Innovation and creativity are powerful drivers of legacy, particularly for those who seek to change industries, reshape culture, or advance human knowledge. People often perceive creativity as a spontaneous, unpredictable force, but in reality, discipline plays a crucial role in it. The most innovative thinkers—whether they are scientists, artists, or entrepreneurs—are those who have applied discipline to their creative processes, allowing them to produce work that leaves an imprint on the world.

Take, for example, the legacy of Thomas Edison, one of the most prolific inventors in history. Edison's famous quote, "Genius is 1% inspiration and 99% perspiration," highlights the role of discipline in innovation. While Edison is often remembered for his creativity, it was his disciplined approach to experimentation and problem-solving that allowed him to bring so many of his ideas to life. He famously tested thousands of materials before discovering the right filament for the light bulb, demonstrating an extraordinary level of persistence and discipline in the pursuit of his vision.

Similarly, we remember artists such as Leonardo da Vinci, Pablo Picasso, and Michelangelo not only for their talent but also for their disciplined work ethic. They dedicated numerous hours to perfecting their skills, refining their methods, and exploring the limits of their artistic mediums. It was this discipline that allowed them to produce a body of work that continues to influence and inspire generations long after their deaths.

In the world of business, innovators like Steve Jobs and Jeff Bezos applied discipline to their visionary ideas, creating products and companies that reshaped industries and changed the way we live. Jobs's relentless focus on design and user experience, paired with his disciplined approach to product development, made Apple one of the most iconic companies in the world. Similarly, Bezos' disciplined focus on customer satisfaction and long-term growth has made Amazon a dominant force in global commerce.

These examples show that discipline is not the antithesis of creativity but its enabler. It allows innovators to take their flashes of inspiration and turn them into tangible, lasting contributions. Without discipline, even the most brilliant ideas would remain unrealized, and the legacies of these outstanding minds would not have endured.

Discipline in Community and Social Impact

Another important aspect of building a legacy is the impact one has on their community or society as a whole. Many individuals make a lasting impression not through personal wealth or fame but through their disciplined dedication to service, social justice, or humanitarian causes. Whether it's through activism, philanthropy, or community-building, discipline is what allows these individuals to create meaningful, long-term change.

Consider the legacy of Mother Teresa, who spent decades working with the poorest and most vulnerable people in Calcutta, India. Her work was not glamorous, nor did it offer immediate rewards. Instead, it required immense discipline, both physically and emotionally, to care for those in desperate need, day after day, for the majority of her life. Her disciplined commitment to her cause has profoundly impacted the world, inspiring countless others to engage in humanitarian work.

Similarly, individuals like Martin Luther King Jr. and Nelson Mandela left legacies rooted in social justice and equality. Their disciplined approach to activism, which often involved enduring imprisonment, harassment, and personal sacrifice, was crucial in achieving civil rights reforms that continue to benefit society today. Their discipline in organizing, advocating, and leading movements for justice created lasting social change and cemented their legacies as icons of human rights.

Discipline in community service also extends to those who work behind the scenes to improve their local communities—volunteers, educators, healthcare workers, and activists who dedicate their lives to helping others. These individuals may not seek recognition, but their disciplined commitment to their work creates ripples of positive change that extend far beyond their immediate actions. Often, the lives they've touched and the communities they've strengthened bear witness to their legacy.

Building a legacy through social impact requires the discipline to remain committed to a cause, even when progress is slow or the obstacles seem insurmountable. It's about showing up consistently, doing the hard work, and remaining dedicated to the greater good. In this way, discipline becomes a force for collective transformation, creating legacies that benefit not just individuals but society as a whole.

Discipline in Family and Personal Legacy

While much of the focus on legacy revolves around public achievements, the legacy individuals leave within their families and personal relationships is equally important. Discipline plays a central role in building a personal legacy, as it allows individuals to uphold values, traditions, and lessons that can be passed down through generations.

Family legacies are often built through the discipline of consistent effort and care. Parents, for example, leave legacies through the time and energy they invest in raising and educating their children. Discipline is required to model positive values, teach life skills, and provide stability, even in the face of life's challenges. The lessons taught through disciplined parenting—such as the importance of hard work, integrity, and perseverance—can shape the lives of children and grandchildren, influencing future generations.

Similarly, the discipline of maintaining strong relationships with family members and loved ones creates a legacy of connection, support, and love. Whether it's through nurturing family bonds, providing guidance, or acting as a source of strength during difficult times, individuals build personal legacies through their disciplined commitment to their relationships.

In addition to the familial legacy, individuals leave behind personal legacies through their character and actions. A disciplined person who lives with integrity, generosity, and kindness can inspire those around them, leaving an eternal mark on family, friends, and colleagues. These intangible legacies, while less visible than public achievements, often hold the most meaning for those who personally knew the individual.

Discipline and the Concept of a Living Legacy

A legacy is often thought of as something that is built over a lifetime and fully realized after one's death. However, the concept of a living legacy emphasizes the idea that individuals can create a meaningful impact throughout their lives, not just at the end of them. A living legacy is about making a difference in real-time, contributing to the world in ways that are felt today and will continue to resonate in the future.

Discipline is central to the idea of a living legacy. By consistently acting in alignment with one's values, maintaining a focus on long-term impact, and staying committed to meaningful work, individuals can create a living legacy that grows and evolves throughout their lifetime. Whether through mentorship, leadership, creative contributions, or community service, a living legacy is built through disciplined actions that benefit others now while also laying the foundation for a lasting legacy in the future.

One's choices and actions dynamically and continuously shape a living legacy. Discipline ensures that individuals stay aligned with their purpose and values, making incremental contributions over time that build a cumulative and profound impact. For example, a teacher may create a living legacy by instilling knowledge and inspiration in students year after year. A business leader may build a company culture rooted in ethics and innovation that continues to influence employees and customers long after they have stepped down.

By embracing discipline, individuals can ensure that the legacy they are building aligns with their true self and brings value to others in real time. A living legacy is not about waiting until the end of life to reflect on what has been accomplished—it's about consistently acting in ways that contribute to the betterment of others, whether in small, everyday acts or in larger, visionary projects.

The Role of Discipline in Building Ethical Legacies

One of the most important aspects of legacy is how people are remembered for their character, values, and integrity. An ethical legacy is built on the disciplined adherence to principles and doing what is right, even when it's difficult. Not only do we remember many individuals throughout history for their achievements, but also for the ethical standards they upheld in the process.

For instance, individuals like Mahatma Gandhi and Rosa Parks left legacies not only because of their actions but also because they were guided by a strong moral compass and an unwavering commitment to justice. Their discipline in maintaining their ethical beliefs, even under tremendous pressure, ensured that their legacies would be remembered as examples of integrity and courage.

Discipline in ethics means being consistent in your actions, treating others with respect, and standing by your values, regardless of external pressures. For instance, in the business world, leaders who uphold a disciplined commitment to ethical practices, even when it may be more profitable to take shortcuts, establish a legacy of trust and respect. Their businesses are often remembered for their integrity, which can have long-lasting positive impacts not just on profits but also on industry standards and social progress.

Personal relationships also require ethical discipline. People who consistently show kindness, honesty, and fairness in their interactions with others are remembered not only for what they accomplished but also for the way they treated people along the way. An ethical legacy is about the values that guided the process, not just the results.

Legacy and the Discipline of Reflection

Building a meaningful legacy requires regular reflection. Discipline is not just about what we do, but also about how much time we spend thinking about whether our actions match our values and goals. Reflection allows individuals to assess their progress, make adjustments, and ensure that they are on the path to leaving the legacy they truly desire.

Many successful individuals make time for self-reflection a regular part of their discipline. Whether through journaling, meditation, or quiet introspection, they assess their decisions, actions, and their impact on others. This disciplined practice of reflection helps them stay aligned with their goals and make course corrections when necessary.

Reflection also provides an opportunity to consider the impact of one's work and relationships. Those who think about their actions are more likely to make a meaningful impact because they are deliberate about their legacy. RDisciplined individuals use reflection to stay purposeful and deliberate in their actions, rather than allowing life to pass by in a series of reactive decisions.

Through reflection, individuals can ask important questions: "Am I living in a way that reflects my values?" "Am I contributing to the lives of others in a positive and lasting way?" "What changes can I make today to ensure I leave behind a legacy I am proud of?" These questions, answered honestly and with discipline, allow individuals to live in a way that creates a legacy of integrity, purpose, and positive impact.

Building a Legacy of Resilience

Resilience is a key quality of individuals who leave lasting legacies. CChallenges, setbacks, and failures are common in life, yet it is the disciplined perseverance of individuals who create legacies that inspires others. Resilience is the ability to keep moving forward, to continue striving toward your goals, and to maintain your values in the face of adversity.

Not only did their achievements shape the legacies of figures like Abraham Lincoln, Nelson Mandela, and Frida Kahlo, but their resilience also played a crucial role. Before becoming one of America's most revered presidents, Lincoln faced numerous political defeats. Mandela spent 27 years in prison before emerging as a global leader for peace and reconciliation. Frida Kahlo endured significant physical pain and personal hardships, yet created art that continues to resonate with millions around the world. In each case, their legacy is as much about their perseverance through hardship as it is about their accomplishments.

Resilience requires discipline because it involves staying committed to your goals even when the path is difficult. It means continuing to take action, no matter how slow the progress might be, and refusing to be deterred by failure or disappointment. Resilient individuals build legacies not because they never experienced setbacks, but because they had the discipline to keep going when others might have given up.

Moreover, resilient legacies are often the most inspiring. When others witness someone overcoming adversity and staying true to their purpose, it inspires them to pursue a similar path. The disciplined resilience of one individual can create a ripple effect, inspiring future generations to persevere in the face of challenges and build legacies of their own.

Creating Your Legacy Through Discipline

Building a meaningful legacy is not an overnight process; it requires a lifetime of disciplined effort, consistent values, and intentional actions. Whether your legacy is in leadership, innovation, creativity, social impact, or personal relationships, discipline is the common thread that ties it all together.

As we've seen from the stories of great leaders, innovators, and everyday individuals, discipline enables us to not only achieve personal success but also to contribute to the world in ways that will last long after we are gone. It allows us to turn our passions into meaningful work, to navigate challenges with resilience, and to leave a mark that is reflective of our true values.

Ultimately, the legacy you build is up to you. It starts with your daily choices, habits, values, and discipline. By living with purpose, acting with integrity, and remaining committed to your long-term vision, you can build a legacy that reflects not only your achievements but also the positive impact you've had on the lives of others.

Discipline is key to ensuring your legacy is about who you were and how you made the world better, not just what you did.

Chapter 10

Embracing Discipline as a Lifelong Journey

The Lifelong Nature of Discipline

Throughout this book, we've explored the profound impact of discipline on various aspects of life—personal growth, professional success, health, creativity, leadership, and legacy. The common thread in all these areas is the understanding that discipline is not a one-time decision or a fleeting effort; it is a continuous process, a journey that unfolds over the course of a lifetime.

Discipline is not a destination; it is a skill you develop over time. It's an essential quality that underpins long-term success, personal growth, and fulfillment. Embracing discipline as a lifelong journey means recognizing that the pursuit of goals, whether they are related to career, relationships, health, or personal development, requires consistent effort, perseverance, and self-awareness.

Importantly, discipline is not about perfection. Life is full of unexpected events, and no one consistently follows their plans. However, those who embrace discipline understand that setbacks are part of the process. Moments of failure or distraction do not discourage them; instead, they use these experiences as opportunities to learn, adjust, and strengthen their resolve.

The lifelong journey of discipline is one of ongoing growth and development. As you evolve, so do your goals, priorities, and challenges. The discipline that helped you achieve one milestone will need to be adapted and expanded as you move toward new ones. Embracing this process with openness and curiosity is key to staying committed to the discipline that drives long-term success.

The Interconnected Nature of Discipline

One of the most powerful lessons about discipline is its interconnectedness with other areas of life. We often think of discipline in isolated terms—discipline in work, discipline in health, and discipline in relationships—but the truth is that discipline in one area often strengthens discipline in others.

For example, developing discipline in maintaining a regular exercise routine can foster greater mental clarity and energy, which in turn enhances your productivity at work. Likewise, cultivating discipline in managing your time and finances can reduce stress, allowing you to focus more effectively on personal goals and relationships. The more disciplined you become in one area of life, the more you create a positive ripple effect that enhances other aspects of your life.

This interconnectedness also means that when discipline falters in one area, it can affect other parts of your life. For example, neglecting self-care or allowing procrastination to take over can lead to decreased focus and motivation in other areas. Recognizing this holistic nature of discipline encourages a more balanced and integrated approach to self-improvement.

Ultimately, discipline is about creating harmony in your life. Your actions align with your highest values and long-term vision, bringing consistency and intentionality to everything you do. By embracing discipline as an integrated part of your life, you can achieve balance and fulfillment in multiple areas simultaneously.

Discipline and the Power of Small Habits

Another key insight from the journey of discipline is the power of small habits. We often think that major achievements require massive, transformative actions, but in reality, the most significant progress often comes from small, consistent habits. Whether it's writing a few hundred words each day, exercising for 30 minutes, or setting aside a few minutes for mindfulness, these small, daily actions accumulate over time and lead to profound results.

The beauty of small habits is that they are manageable. By focusing on small, disciplined actions, you reduce the overwhelming pressure that often accompanies large goals. Instead of worrying about how you'll achieve an ambitious target, you can simply focus on the task at hand—taking one small, disciplined step forward each day.

Over time, these small habits compound. As you build momentum, each action reinforces the next, and before you know it, you've made significant progress toward your goals. This approach not only fosters discipline but also helps prevent burnout, as it emphasizes sustainability and long-term consistency over short bursts of effort.

The power of small habits reminds us that discipline is not about dramatic changes—it's about consistency. It's the day-to-day commitment to showing up, putting in the work, and staying focused on your priorities. By embracing the power of small habits, you can make discipline a natural and sustainable part of your life.

The Role of Discipline in Resilience

Discipline and resilience are deeply connected. A disciplined individual is capable of navigating life's challenges with grace and determination. Discipline provides the structure and mindset needed to keep going when things become tough. Whether you're facing professional setbacks, personal challenges, or moments of self-doubt, discipline is what helps you stay on track and push forward.

Resilience, in turn, strengthens discipline. As you overcome obstacles and learn from failures, you become more disciplined in your approach to future challenges. You develop a more profound understanding of what it takes to stay committed, even in the face of adversity. This feedback loop between discipline and resilience creates a powerful cycle of growth, allowing you to navigate life's inevitable challenges with greater confidence and determination.

Disciplined individuals embrace challenges head-on, understanding each one as a chance to fortify themselves, acquire fresh insights, and enhance their strategies. This resilience is a key component of long-term success, as it allows you to persist when others might give up.

Discipline and Flexibility: The Balance Structure and Adaptation

While discipline provides structure, it's important to recognize that it is not rigid. In fact, one of the most powerful aspects of discipline is the ability to remain flexible and adaptable. Those who are disciplined know how to adjust their approach without losing sight of their long-term goals, as life rarely unfolds according to plan.

This balance between structure and flexibility is essential for maintaining discipline over the long term. It's important to create routines and habits that support your goals, but it's equally important to be willing to adapt those routines when circumstances change. Flexibility allows you to maintain your commitment to discipline without becoming discouraged by unexpected obstacles or shifts in priorities.

For example, if a disciplined runner faces an injury, they might adapt their routine to focus on strength training or rehabilitation exercises. Being adaptable helps them stay on track with their overall objective of fitness and health, even if it means temporarily changing certain habits.

Flexibility in discipline also applies to your long-term vision. As you grow and evolve, your goals may change. The disciplined individual is not afraid to reevaluate their priorities and shift their focus when necessary. This ability to adapt ensures that discipline remains a tool for growth and success, rather than a rigid set of rules that limit creativity or personal evolution.

The Legacy of Discipline

As we explored in the previous chapter, discipline is central to building a lasting legacy. When you consistently live with discipline, you achieve your personal and professional goals and leave behind a legacy that can inspire others. Whether it's through leadership, creative contributions, or the way you've touched the lives of those around you, the discipline you practice today creates ripples that extend far beyond your life.

The legacy of discipline is built on the cumulative impact of your actions over time. It's not about grand gestures or isolated moments of success—it's about the day-to-day commitment to living with purpose, integrity, and intentionality. Your discipline shapes your future and that of those you influence, mentor, or lead.

In the end, the legacy you leave is a reflection of how you lived. Discipline helps you live by your values, make a difference, and reach your most important goals. You establish a lasting legacy through discipline.

Embracing Discipline as a Lifelong Journey

As you move forward from reading this book, remember that discipline is not a destination—it's a journey. It's a skill that you will continue to develop and refine throughout your life. Some days, discipline will come easily, while other days it may feel like a struggle. But by embracing discipline as a core part of who you are, you will find that the rewards of persistence, resilience, and commitment far outweigh the challenges.

Embrace the small steps. Embrace the setbacks. Embrace the process of becoming more disciplined each day, knowing that every action you take is moving you closer to your long-term goals. Whether you are striving to build a career, improve your health, create something meaningful, or leave a legacy that lasts, discipline will be your greatest ally on the journey.

By cultivating discipline, you are choosing to live with intention and purpose. You are choosing to prioritize what truly matters, even when it's difficult. You are choosing to invest in your growth, your success, and your legacy.

The journey of discipline is one that never truly ends—but it is a journey that is deeply rewarding, full of growth, and filled with the potential for greatness. Embrace discipline, not as a burden, but as the key to unlocking your fullest potential and living a life of purpose and fulfillment.

Conclusion

Long-term success, personal growth, and fulfillment are all based on discipline. It is the quiet, consistent force that drives us forward when motivation fades, when challenges arise, and when distractions beckon. Discipline is not about grand gestures or extraordinary willpower; it is about showing up every day and doing the work that matters, one small step at a time.

As we've explored in this book, discipline touches every area of our lives. It is the key to unlocking your potential, building resilience, and achieving your most ambitious goals. Whether it's in your career, health, relationships, or creative pursuits, discipline is the thread that ties together effort and results. It empowers you to overcome procrastination, stay focused in the face of distractions, and keep moving forward even when the path is unclear.

The road of discipline is not always easy, but it is always worth it. The greatest achievements, the most meaningful legacies, and the deepest sense of fulfillment come from a life lived with purpose and discipline. Through discipline, we learn to be patient with ourselves, to embrace the process of growth, and to celebrate the progress we make along the way.

As you move forward, remember that discipline is a practice, not a destination. It is a lifelong journey that will evolve as you evolve, but the principles remain the same: consistent effort, resilience in the face of setbacks, and a commitment to your long-term vision. With discipline as your guide, there are no limits to what you can achieve.

So, as you close this book, ask yourself: How can I apply the principles of discipline to my life? What small steps can I take today to move closer to my goals? How can I cultivate resilience, adaptability, and focus to create the life I truly want?

The answers to these questions will shape your path forward. With discipline, you have the power to achieve your dreams, make a lasting difference, and live a life that reflects your highest values. Embrace the journey, stay committed to your vision, and trust that the disciplined steps you take today will lead to a future full of purpose, success, and fulfillment.

Thank you for embarking on this journey of discipline. May it serve as your compass on the road ahead, guiding you toward the life you are destined to create.

About the Author

Benjamin M. Noynay is a passionate and dedicated Music Teacher and a Business Coach based in Melbourne, Australia.

As a Music Teacher, Ben incorporates the principles of empowerment into his lessons, which leads to an effective collaboration with his students in a way that opens the doors of ownership, responsibility, and accountability for both of them. Once officially enrolled as Ben's student, you will begin a challenging yet enjoyable journey of learning music with a focused objective of achieving excellence by developing and maximizing your God-given gifts and talents and eventually converting them into skillful performances that you can share with the world.

As a Business Coach, Ben focuses on teaching and guiding his clients on how to grow their business by using the tools and resources of RIGHT Coaching Systems. He helps them achieve both their business and personal goals in order to enjoy an abundant, well-balanced, and fulfilling lifestyle. As the founder of RIGHT Coaching Systems, Ben sets high standards on how he conducts his business based on Respect, Integrity, Gratitude, Honesty, and Trust. He believes that you can be a successful business owner and a good person at the same time. Once your coaching relationship with Ben starts, he will be there with you every step of the way until you achieve your goals.

www.ingramcontent.com/pod-product-compliance
Lightning Source LLC
Chambersburg PA
CBHW071959290426
44109CB00018B/2074